T0341611

THE MAKING

=== OF A ===

PROPHET

Practical Advice for
Developing Your Prophetic Voice

JENNIFER LECLAIRE

Chosen
a division of Baker Publishing Group
Minneapolis, Minnesota

Published by Chosen Books
11400 Hampshire Avenue South
Minneapolis, Minnesota 55438
www.chosenbooks.com

Chosen Books is a division of
Baker Publishing Group, Grand Rapids, Michigan

Printed in the United States of America

Library of Congress Cataloging-in-Publication Data
LeClaire, Jennifer (Jennifer L.)
    The making of a prophet : practical advice for developing your prophetic voice / Jennifer LeClaire.
    pages cm
    Summary: "Leading prophetic voice Jennifer LeClaire offers expert advice on developing the prophetic gift, from the initial call through the intense making process into maturity"—Provided by publisher.
    ISBN 978-0-8007-9562-7 (pbk. : alk. paper)
    1. Prophecy—Christianity. 2. Gifts, Spiritual. I. Title.
BR115.P8L43 2014
234′.13—dc23   2013032774

Cover design by Dan Pitts

Baker Publishing Group publications use paper produced from sustainable forestry practices and post-consumer waste whenever possible.

"*The Making of a Prophet* is a clean read, filled with good information expressed in a refreshingly simple and direct style that every reader will enjoy. Jennifer LeClaire beautifully covers a wide range of issues that affect prophetic ministry both biblically and with practical wisdom."

R. Loren Sandford, senior pastor,
New Song Church and Ministries, Denver

"Jennifer LeClaire has written *The Making of a Prophet* for this hour! Whether you just have some small inkling or have ministered a long time in the prophetic, there is much wisdom to be mined like treasure from its page. *The Making of a Prophet* is destined to be a classic for generations to come."

Cindy Jacobs,
Generals International, Dallas

"Jennifer LeClaire has done an excellent job presenting *The Making of a Prophet*. This book is a must-read for every saint of God."

Dr. Bill Hamon, bishop,
Christian International Ministries Network (CIMN);
Christian International Apostolic Network (CIAN);
Christian International Global Network (CIGN);
author, *The Day of the Saints* and ten other books

"Jennifer LeClaire answers the question that has been on the hearts and minds of countless Christians: 'Am I called to the prophetic, and if so, what do I do?' Whatever the sacrifice, take *The Making of a Prophet* into your hands and into your heart. I can assure you, it will not let you go until your questions are answered."

Steve Hill, evangelist,
Steve Hill Ministries, Dallas;
author, *Spiritual Avalanche* and others

This book is dedicated to
all the prophets who refuse to compromise.

Contents

Foreword

Jennifer LeClaire has done an excellent job presenting *The Making of a Prophet*. I can verify the truths she presents, for I have functioned as a prophet for the sixty years of my ordained ministry and developed the 10 Ms for determining true and false ministers: *manhood, ministry, message, maturity, marriage, methods, manners, money, morality* and *motive*. These are the areas God works on in the making of a prophet. They are also the areas a prophet must keep in godly order to maintain and mature in his or her life and ministry.

Jennifer is accurate in saying that not everyone who prophesies is a prophet. There are five areas or levels of prophetic ministry:

1. The spirit of prophecy—Jesus' testifying to others through prophetic speaking (see Revelation 19:10)
2. The gift of prophecy (see 1 Corinthians 12:10)
3. The prophetic presbytery for laying on hands and prophecy for ordination (see 1 Timothy 4:14)
4. Prophetic preaching
5. The gift of prophet (see Ephesians 4:11)

This book will help you discover whether you are a saint functioning in the spirit of prophecy, on which level every saint born of the Spirit may prophesy (see 1 Corinthians 14:1, 31), whether you are manifesting the gift of prophecy or whether you are called to be a prophet. This book is a must-read for every saint of God.

God bless you, Jennifer, for allowing the Lord to work in your 10 Ms and make you a prophet to the Body of Christ and the world.

Dr. Bill Hamon, bishop,
Christian International Ministries Network (CIMN);
Christian International Apostolic Network (CIAN);
Christian International Global Network (CIGN);
author, *The Day of the Saints* and ten other books

Acknowledgments

Many thanks to Jane Campbell, editorial director of Chosen Books, for believing in the importance of raising up pure prophetic voices in these days. I pray this book will forward that cause.

Many thanks to prophetic pioneers who authored many books on various aspects of the prophetic ministry. I learned from so many, including Dr. Bill Hamon, T. Austin Sparks and John and Paula Sandford. Their now-classic materials continue to teach many. I pray that this will build on the foundation they laid.

Lastly, many thanks to my early apostolic and prophetic mentors who helped me understand what it means to go through the making process.

1

Is God Calling Me into Prophetic Ministry?

When I got saved in the county jail, I had no idea there were modern-day prophets proclaiming the word of God to ordinary people. Sure, I was familiar with fortune-tellers and palm readers—I had even wasted hard-earned money on their foolish predictions—but real prophets? People who serve as literal mouthpieces for God Almighty?

Then it happened. Within days of accepting Jesus as my Savior, I encountered a bona fide prophetic ministry. A prophet visited the jail faithfully every week and delivered prophetic words to several women. He foretold who would be set free and who would serve longer sentences. He also laid bare the secrets of our hearts and drew us closer to Jesus. His accuracy seemed flawless.

Soon, I began hearing the still, small voice of the Holy Spirit in my own heart. I developed keen awareness of things that I knew only God Himself could have revealed. The Holy Spirit told me, for example, that I would be released on the fortieth day. That seemed impossible. Even though I protested my innocence—a police officer had falsely accused me of striking her because I had asked her not to arrest my boyfriend—I had been denied bond twice, and the disagreeable judge was going to be on vacation well past the forty-day mark. My case was difficult to prove—it was the police officer's word against mine—but the prosecutor was pushing hard for a five-year sentence.

God must have given me the gift of faith, because I was so confident about that prophetic word—which the Holy Spirit confirmed repeatedly—that I was emboldened. During a collect call to my crying mother, I told her with assurance that I was innocent and would be released on the fortieth day. I told my cell mates that I would be released on the fortieth day. Like the apostle Paul, I believed God that it would be just as it was told to me (see Acts 27:25).

I was released on the fortieth day, my innocence affirmed, without my ever standing before a judge.

A Prophetic Announcement

Despite that supernatural event, it took me a while to connect the dots and see the prophetic calling on my life. For years I continued to hear the voice of the Lord in my spirit with great accuracy. I even heard the audible voice of the Lord one time while on my knees crying out to Him during a crisis. But it never occurred to me that I had any particular prophetic gifting. I thought it was the normal Christian experience.

Then came a prophetic announcement that opened my eyes and dropped my jaw. It was during a time of spiritual warfare. I did not feel like going to church that morning, but I went anyway. At the end of the service an apostle prophesied this over me: "You are a voice of governing authority . . . a voice of governing authority. . . . I release that voice now, in the name of Jesus!" Well, I had no idea what "a voice of governing authority" was, but I accepted the prophetic word. I went home and tried to find something about it in Scripture.

As I opened my Bible, the Lord supernaturally took me to three instances in the gospels where John the Baptist speaks of "the voice of one crying in the wilderness." When I opened my Bible, randomly, Matthew 3:3 was staring at me. After I read it, I flipped ahead and Mark 1:3 was illumined on the page. I flipped some pages again and the Bible fell open to Luke 3:4, which offered the same account of John the Baptist for a third time. It was what a mature prophet later described as a "three-fold witness" from Scripture. I kept reading those verses and studying the call of John the Baptist, along with the government of God and authority.

It is clear to me now that the Holy Spirit was revealing a call to prophetic ministry. At the time I was yet unsure. The thought of a prophetic call was overwhelming and even scary. I kept all of this to myself and started searching for books I could read on prophetic ministry. Most of the books I read did not help much because they were about hearing the voice of God. (Hearing the voice of God was not my problem; how was I to speak it out?) I finally stumbled onto Bill Hamon's *Prophets and Personal Prophecy*. Much of it was like glimpses of my own experiences on paper. After I read his trilogy on the subject, the Holy Spirit spoke to my heart and confirmed my call into prophetic ministry.

How Can I Know I Am Called?

There is a lot of confusion regarding the call into prophetic ministry. Many Christians are looking for confirmation. I get email frequently from people asking, "How can I tell if I am called to be a prophet?" This is an important question. In order to walk worthy of your calling, you first need to be confident God has called you. Once you are sure, you can count the cost and decide whether or not to embrace the spiritual battle that lies ahead.

Although I generally discount "checklists" that tell you whether or not you are an apostle or prophet or operate in some other ministry gifting, there are practical ways for believers to confirm a prophetic calling in their own hearts, which we will discuss in this chapter. And it is safe to say that if you are called into prophetic ministry, mature leaders around you will recognize that call eventually.

There are exceptions to that last point. Some pastors are too insecure to recognize the gifts and callings of those in their midst. But if you are called into prophetic ministry, be assured that people will discern that call in due season. You do not have to make an announcement, try to show off your prophetic gifts or otherwise strive to let people know. God will make it apparent in His time. In fact, waiting for Him to reveal your gifting in public ministry is part of *the making process*, the course of Holy Spirit training, teaching and practical experience that you will learn about through the pages of this book.

So, are you called into prophetic ministry? Here are two important points to help you address this question.

First, perhaps you received a prophetic word announcing your calling. That could well have been an authentic word, but take the time to look for further confirmation. I have seen prophetic words send sincere believers on spiritual goose chases for gifts and callings that Jesus did not impart. It is sad to see people hold tightly to an erroneous word they believe is genuine and miss God's true call for their lives.

Second, perhaps you are consistently seeing revelatory gifts—such as words of wisdom, words of knowledge and discerning of spirits—manifesting in your ministry. That gives you a hint of your Kingdom vocation. It is actually a better indication that you are called to prophetic ministry than an announcement spoken, say, at the altar by a visiting prophet.

In the King James Version of Ephesians 4:1, Paul urges us to "walk worthy of the vocation wherewith [we] are called."

That word *vocation* gives us insight into how a calling of God manifests. Another word for *vocation* is *occupation*.

Think about it this way: Doctors are educated and trained to practice medicine. That is what they do day in and day out. And they do not just practice medicine at work. They practice medicine at home when someone in the family gets sick. They practice medicine in a restaurant if someone passes out and they hear the cry "Is there a doctor in the house?" Even when doctors retire, they remember the Hippocratic Oath they swore to uphold. Whether they are in the church, the marketplace or the home front, doctors are doctors.

Likewise, if you are called as a prophet, it is an occupation. You cannot turn off the instinct to stand in the office of the prophet any more than a physician can turn off the instinct to help people heal. If you are called to prophetic ministry, you will walk in the revelatory gifts as a way of life, not just occasionally. You will feel the unction to walk in prophetic gifts consistently.

Manifestations of Modern-Day Ministry

If you have this ministry gift of being a prophet, what might it look like? We will study this in greater detail in later chapters, but, generally, the purpose of prophecy is to reveal the heart, mind and will of God.

Modern-day prophetic ministry is more than the usual public perception. It is more than prophesying over people in prayer lines. It is more than having dreams, visions and angelic visitations. Far more. Modern-day prophets are reformers, like John the Baptist. Prophetic ministry should bring positive change and hope. A reformation mindset is part of what it means to be prophetic. Prophets have reformation in their DNA.

Modern-day prophets are called to prepare a people for the Lord by pointing them to an intimate relationship with Jesus (see John 3:29), equipping them to discern His voice (see

Ephesians 4:11–12), speaking words of warning or correction that God gives them (see Matthew 3:2–3) and standing in the gap between man and God (see Ezekiel 22:30). Usually this latter function takes place through intercession. Not all intercessors are prophets, but all prophets are intercessors. It is part of the prophetic priestly duty to make intercession. The first time you see the word *prophet* in the Bible, it is in connection with intercession (see Genesis 20:7). You cannot separate the prophet from prayer because prayer is the prophet's connection with God and His will.

Modern-day prophetic ministry involves turning the hearts of the fathers toward the sons and the hearts of the sons toward the fathers (see Malachi 4:5–6). The Amplified translation calls this turning a "reconciliation produced by repentance of the ungodly." Prophetic ministry, thus, turns the hearts of believers toward the matters of the Father's heart. Often, that means a cry for repentance as modern-day prophetic ministry works to separate the holy from the profane (see Ezekiel 42:20).

If you are called as a prophet, you will feel moved to root out and to pull down and to destroy and to throw down and to build and to plant (see Jeremiah 1:10). Intense spiritual warfare will be a frequent reality in your life. You will have a sense—a "knowing"—that you are being called to walk a narrower path than some around you. You will feel a sense of duty to honor God's will and be crushed with godly sorrow when you misstep.

Are All Prophets?

Again, not everyone who receives a word about having a prophetic calling is truly called into the fivefold ministry named in Ephesians 4:11. The Bible states clearly in this verse that Jesus "gave some" to be prophets, and Paul asks rhetorically, "Are all prophets?" (1 Corinthians 12:29). Just because you get prophetic revelation or move in prophecy—even if you do these things frequently—does not necessarily mean you are a prophet. Anyone who is filled with the Holy Spirit can exercise the gift of prophecy as He wills (see 1 Corinthians 12:7–11).

Paul told the church at Corinth to "desire earnestly [covet] to prophesy" (1 Corinthians 14:39). Some young or inexperienced ones confuse that with coveting the office of the prophet. I cannot tell you how many on-fire Christians I have met who call themselves prophets yet have no discernible call on their lives—or how much email I get from people asking me how they can achieve the office of prophet.

There is a huge difference between willingness to be used by God to prophesy—the gift Paul commended to the Church—and coveting the office of prophet. Prophecy is a gift of the Spirit imparted to the Spirit-filled believer, and we should "earnestly desire" to manifest that gift for His glory. The Amplified Bible's rendering of 1 Corinthians 14:39 clarifies the proper motive: "Earnestly desire and set your hearts on prophesying (on being inspired to preach and teach and to interpret God's will and purpose)." Every believer should be eager to prophesy because it edifies, comforts and exhorts the Church—and the Church needs edification, exhortation and comfort.

The office of the prophet is quite a different thing. Jesus anoints prophets and sets them in the Church according to His will:

> [Jesus] gave some to be to be apostles, some prophets, some evangelists, and some pastors and teachers, for the equipping of the saints for the work of ministry, for the edifying of the body of Christ, till we all come to the unity of the faith and of the knowledge of the Son of God, to a perfect man, to the measure of the stature of the fullness of Christ.
>
> Ephesians 4:11–13

You cannot make yourself a prophet. Jesus has to call you to this office—and even if He does, you still cannot "make" yourself a prophet. God has to make you. If you are not called to prophetic ministry, there is nothing you can do to walk in that anointing. And if you try to force Jesus' hand, you will simply invite the enemy in to offer you a false anointing that could ultimately lead you to a fiery fate.

I urge you not to jump to the conclusion that you are a prophet just because someone prophesies a calling over you or because you can cast out a devil or because you are a powerful prayer warrior. I assure you, if you are truly called into prophetic ministry, God will make that abundantly clear to you at the right time. Yes, He may use others to announce or confirm your prophetic calling. But He might just deal with you privately for years as He unlocks the mystery over your life one step at a time.

There are more than a few in the Body of Christ carrying titles without fruit in ministry because God has not anointed them in those particular areas. This seems especially true with the prophetic. Some chase the prophetic office like an idol. Others are trying to walk out erroneous prophetic words. Still others have sincerely misunderstood God's call in their hearts out of a holy passion to serve Jesus. Jesus needs every believer in his or her proper role. He needs those who are called to be prophets to be confident in their call—and those who are called elsewhere to step into their true and equally important functions in the Body.

Rather than looking with natural eyes, look through the eyes of the Spirit. God calls some young and others old. Either way, if you are called into prophetic ministry, God has likely been preparing you to walk in this vocation even before announcing, confirming and activating it.

2

I'm Called—Now What?

When God first calls you into prophetic ministry, it is exhilarating; it is humbling; it is scary. It is an awesome assignment—almost overwhelming when you grasp the responsibility of serving in the end times as a mouthpiece for the God of the universe. The prophetic calling brings with it temptation toward pride in some and true fear of the Lord in others.

If your pride trumps your patience, you will rush headlong into prophetic ministry without God's clear commissioning. If you are not sensitive to His ways, you can move out of His timing. Understand this: There is a period of time between the calling and the commissioning. That time could be long or short. Regardless, what some call "the making process" of a prophet does not end when you are commissioned for service. It never truly ends. You will always be gaining deeper revelation of who God is and how He wants to use you.

Typically God will begin using you in small ways before launching you into more visible prophetic ministry. This is for your own safety as you learn and grow in the gifts and in your character. Think about it for a minute. *The enemy is opposed to the will of God. Prophets speak forth the will of God.* That puts a target on your back. If you run out ahead of God's grace, you open yourself to more warfare—and you will see plenty of warfare without inviting the enemy to take a cheap shot.

Responding to the Prophetic Calling

So how should you respond to the prophetic calling? Whether you received a prophetic word in a public prayer line or heard the still, small voice of God in your prayer closet, the appropriate response can be summed up in a single word: *humility*. Begin cultivating humility in your heart immediately, and combine your budding humility with willingness and obedience that will carry you with integrity to the finish line of your prophetic race.

When my prophetic call was revealed, a mature prophet in my local church asked my best friend how I was "taking it." She was concerned about me. She had seen too many respond to the prophetic call the wrong way and go off the deep end. The wrong way is anything that resembles pride or arrogance. Prophets are not more important than other members of the Body of Christ; prophets just have a different gift. But it is a gift that appears to some as more exciting, and that can lead to pride.

Sometimes it seems as though half the Body of Christ wants to be a prophet and the other half wants to receive prophetic words. Put another way, there is hunger for the prophetic, but the true prophetic brings warfare. So when some young gun tells me he just received a call into prophetic ministry, I feel like grabbing him, hugging him and saying, "It's going to be all right!" If people knew what they were getting into when they accepted the call, they might stop to count the cost before printing business cards that announce their ministry. True prophetic ministry is not nearly as sensational as many have made it out to be. Most of the real work is done in the prayer closet.

If you have been called as a prophet, purpose in your heart to align your character with Christ's. Commit to consecrating yourself to God at a deeper level, realizing there is a price to pay to walk in true prophetic ministry. Set yourself apart to worship, pray and study the Word more so God can equip you and impart to your heart the revelation of who He is. The revelation of His beauty and the grace of the Holy Spirit will empower you to walk the difficult journey ahead. Decide once and for all that you are willing to do whatever He asks you to do and obey His Word. Let your heart say, "Here am I, Lord! Send me" (see Isaiah 6:8).

Accepting the Responsibility

When you read about the prophetic calls of Moses, Isaiah, Jeremiah and others, you will notice the common theme of humility. When God called Moses to deliver Israel from the bondage of Egypt, he said, "Who am I that I should go to Pharaoh, and that I should bring the children of Israel out of Egypt?" (Exodus 3:11). When God called Isaiah, he considered himself "a man of unclean lips" (Isaiah 6:5). When God called Jeremiah, he said, "Ah, Lord GOD! Behold, I cannot speak, for I am a youth" (Jeremiah 1:6).

Honestly, if you are not overwhelmed by God's call, then you probably think more highly of yourself than you should. As I mentioned earlier, it should be somewhat overwhelming to consider the responsibility of standing in the office of the prophet. God is entrusting you with His secrets (see Amos 3:7).

Shortly after God called me into prophetic ministry, He told me to read Ezekiel 3 and Ezekiel 33. I will never forget it. I was sitting on a bunk bed one night in an open air dorm in Latin America. It was hot and mosquitoes were buzzing around. Everyone was asleep, so I got out my mini-flashlight to read the Word. This is what I read:

"Son of man, I have made you a watchman for the house of Israel; therefore hear a word from My mouth, and give them warning from Me: When I say to the wicked, 'You shall surely die,' and you give him no warning, nor speak to warn the wicked from his wicked way, to save his life, that same wicked man shall die in his iniquity; but his blood I will require at your hand. Yet, if you warn the wicked, and he does not turn from his wickedness, nor from his wicked way, he shall die in his iniquity; but you have delivered your soul."

Ezekiel 3:17

Ezekiel 33 offered a similar message about blowing the trumpet to warn the people. Failing to do so would leave blood on my hands. It was a sobering moment. I realized that God was calling me to the unpopular ministry of "prophetic warning," part of the watchman aspect of prophetic ministry. Many people do not listen to watchmen—and if they do listen, they do not necessarily like what they hear.

God might not be calling you to a strong watchman's ministry. While this manifestation is part of the prophet's call, God directs some prophets toward it more than others. He might give you a different assignment with prophetic utterances that are warmly received by the masses. But that is not usually the case with true prophetic ministry. True prophets do not tend to gain the appreciation of the masses but of the remnant.

Not Despising Small Beginnings

Beyond humility, you will need plenty of patience at the beginning of your prophetic ministry. At first, few people, if any, will recognize the call—and it is usually not wise to announce your fledgling ministry to the world the day after you believe God has called you. That alone displays the lack of maturity required to withstand the spiritual warfare prophets endure.

Still it is easy enough to despise the day of small beginnings in your prophetic ministry. Small beginnings usually start with plenty of questions and very few answers. Small beginnings often come without recognition but with plenty of resistance. Small beginnings are typically uncomfortable, frustrating and discouraging on many levels. Nevertheless, the Bible advises: "Do not despise these small beginnings, for the LORD rejoices to see the work begin" (Zechariah 4:10 NLT).

I remember when God planted a seed in my heart to pray for the nations. I had a large multicolored map on my wall, and I was in awe of the massive opportunities for prophetic intercession. Suddenly, the Lord illuminated a tiny speck of an island on this map, one of the smallest islands in the Caribbean. This was my prayer assignment. I was disappointed! I wanted to storm the heavens over pivotal nations in the earth, but the Lord gave me a small beginning.

It was a lesson in "he who is faithful in what is least is faithful also in much" (Luke 16:10). I prayed faithfully for that tiny nation, its people, its safety, and that the Gospel would break in there and bring salvation. God later began to give me more substantial intercessory assignments and, in 2007, woke me up at midnight to share His heart about America and the coming Great Awakening.

It may be years before God uses you to prophesy over nations. Or He may never use you that way at all. Rest assured that whatever way He begins to use you is important to His eternal purposes. God wants you to be willing and obedient, whether He calls you to stay hidden in a prayer closet all the days of your life or travel the nations with prophetic words to kings. God wants to see you fulfill your prophetic destiny.

All Promotion Comes from God

I also remember when God planted a seed in my heart to have an impact on the nations through the written word. I had the best computer I could afford and plenty of ideas, but no platform. Suddenly, God gave me an opportunity to edit books for other Christian ministers. I did my best to help them prepare their works for publication, hoping one day to write my own Christian books and materials.

Fast-forward just a few years, and my work has been read in almost every nation on the earth. Some has been archived in the Assembly of God's Flower Pentecostal Heritage Center Museum in Springfield, Missouri, and some has been translated into Spanish and Korean. It was a lesson: "If you have not been faithful in what is another man's, who will give you what is your own?" (Luke 16:12). Put another way, when you are faithful over another person's gift, God will let you use your own in a greater way.

If God has called you into prophetic ministry, be prepared to start small so that God can promote you. Never despise the day of lowly beginnings. King David had a small beginning in a field tending sheep, and he experienced more intense warfare than you or I will probably ever experience. Nehemiah rebuilt the wall of Jerusalem with a remnant despite the opposition and the odds. The Bible is full of examples of God calling people just like you and waiting patiently for them to mature so He can use them in a greater way. If that is you right now, then rejoice and stay on the path: "He who calls you is faithful, who also will do it" (1 Thessalonians 5:24).

Once you are confident that you are called into prophetic ministry, you should pray for an attitude of humility and patience. Also prepare for a lifestyle of prayer, fasting and Bible study as you wait for God to reveal the steps along your prophetic journey.

But first, even before that, you must count the cost. Are you prepared to start waging war? Do you understand that there will be persecution? Let's explore that.

3

Are You Willing to Pay the Price?

Jesus gives the prophetic anointing freely to those He calls into prophetic ministry—and the gifts and callings of God are irrevocable, "without repentance" on God's part (Romans 11:29 KJV). In other words, God does not remove the call or the spiritual gifts He gives you even if you are not wholly living for His purposes. He might not be able to use you the way He intended, but since His gifts and callings sprang out of love, He does not take them back. But you pay a price to walk in prophetic ministry with integrity that leads you to your highest calling. You start paying that price during the making process—and that price is usually dear.

If you hope to fulfill God's call and walk in the anointing He has reserved for you without falling into error, you will have to make sacrifices along the way. The question is, Are you willing to pay the price? Do not answer that question until you have counted the cost. If there is a cost to being a true disciple of Christ, then how much more is the cost to be His mouthpiece in an age of culture wars and the persecuted Church! Be realistic about what you may have to give up in order to cooperate with the Spirit and go where He wants to take you.

> "For which of you, intending to build a tower, does not sit down first and count the cost, whether he has enough to finish it—lest, after he has laid the foundation, and is not able to finish, all who see it begin to mock him, saying, 'This man began to build and was not able to finish.' Or what king, going to make war against another king, does not sit down first and consider whether he is able with ten thousand to meet him who comes against him with twenty thousand? Or else, while the other is still a great way off, he sends a delegation and asks conditions of peace."
>
> Luke 14:28–33

Prophets are called to build towers of prayer and to serve as watchmen in the Kingdom of God. Likewise, prophets are led to make war against principalities and powers that are working to block God's will in the earth. Do you see how obedience to the calling comes at a cost? I am convinced that many fallen prophets failed because they did not take the time to consider the price of standing in the office of a prophet or to seek deliverance for themselves before attempting to deliver others.

Before you enter prophetic ministry—and in order to ensure that you are entering prophetic ministry the right way—take the time to count the cost. Consider what impact answering God's call is going to have on your daily life. You might have to change the way you spend your time and whom you spend it with. You might have to change how you spend your money and what you spend it on. You might have to sacrifice many things you love along your journey.

Indeed, sometimes paying the price means giving up close friends (or even family) who are unknowingly hindering God's plans for your life. Other times paying the price means walking away from ministry assignments you enjoy in order to step into the next thing God is calling you to. And paying the price always means giving up wrong mindsets the Holy Spirit exposes in order to embrace truths that will set you free to pursue God's prophetic purposes for your life.

Prophets Who Paid the Price

Jeremiah. Ezekiel. Isaiah. Most New Testament prophets, if we count ourselves among them, will never face the persecution—or ultimately pay even a small percentage of the price—our Old Testament counterparts endured.

Jeremiah was known as the weeping prophet. He delivered the word of the Lord faithfully, and it cost him everything. His family and neighbors turned against him. His peers rejected and reviled him. He was whipped and put into stocks. He was nearly murdered by a priestly flash mob. Hananiah, a false prophet, accused him of lying. He was arrested for treason, flogged and imprisoned in filthy quarters. And he learned that wicked King Jehoiakim had burned his prophetic message that was written on a scroll. Jeremiah eventually became depressed, even cursing the day he was born.

Like today's New Testament prophets, Jeremiah was prophesying into a dark world. People did not want to hear the voice of the Lord—but he refused to remain silent in his generation.

Ezekiel also paid a dear price to obey the Lord's calling as a watchman. Although the prophet Jeremiah never married (see Jeremiah 16:1–4) and the prophet Hosea had to buy his wife out of prostitution (see Hosea 1–3), Ezekiel paid perhaps the greatest price of all when it comes to personal relationships. As part of his prophetic message, Ezekiel had to watch his wife die suddenly and show no grief publicly (see Ezekiel 25:15–18).

Then there are Zechariah and Isaiah, who gave up their very lives to stay true to the message God gave them. Zechariah (an earlier prophet than the one who wrote the book bearing his name) was stoned to death in the courtyard of the Lord's Temple (see 2 Chronicles 24:21), and tradition teaches that Isaiah was sawed in two by King Manasseh. Although it is rare that God calls anyone to such extreme measures, your heart must be willing to pay any price if you hope to walk worthy of your vocation.

Again, you probably will not face anything that even closely resembles what your Old Testament counterparts faced. But you will no doubt suffer persecution, encounter intense spiritual warfare and meet with fiery trials of various kinds as you stand in the office of a prophet. Some seem to pay a greater price than others to walk out their prophetic destinies. Setting your mind ahead of time to be willing to pay any price—knowing that God Himself will repay—is key to fulfilling your prophetic calling.

Consider Job. Job lost his children, his home, his riches. He suffered a painful disease. Job also cursed the day he was born, but he endured the suffering and God repaid him double. The promise is even greater for our generation. Jesus said, "Everyone who has left houses or brothers or sisters or father or mother or wife or children or lands, for My name's sake, shall receive a hundredfold, and inherit eternal life" (Matthew 19:29). There is no price you can pay that God cannot match.

Losing Everything I Worked For

I remember a time in my Christian walk when God asked me a pointed question: *Are you willing to pay the price to go where I want to take you?* Just as I was about to answer "Yes, Lord," He said, *Don't answer without considering the cost.* In obedience, I thought about it, prayed about it and considered it from every angle I could think of, which was obviously limited as compared to God's thoughts. I determined that I was willing to pay the price, even though I did not know exactly what the price was. I went back to the Lord and told Him I was ready and willing. He responded, *You will pay a very dear price.*

This did not scare me, but I knew He was serious. I had no idea what He meant or even how soon I would pay that price, or at least begin paying it. Within months, He changed my associations, my ministry and my life. To obey His call, I had to give up positions, titles, friends, spiritual family and more. It might seem odd, considering what God had told me, but I did not realize at the time what was happening, and it was painful. It was part of that "dear price."

I got clarity about a year later when I was reading Philippians 3. Paul the apostle was explaining that we should have no confidence in the flesh. As I see it, that includes titles, positions, money and anything other than God. Paul wrote how he had plenty of reasons to trust in the flesh. He was circumcised on the eighth day, of the stock of Israel, of the tribe of Benjamin, a Hebrew of Hebrews. Concerning training, he was a Pharisee; concerning zeal, a persecutor of the Church; concerning the righteousness prescribed in the Law, blameless (see verses 4–6).

Paul had a lot going for him under the religious system of the day, but he was willing to pay a dear price to answer God's call. He was willing to forsake all of his status and reputation in exchange for knowing Christ better. Let's listen to his words in Philippians 3:7–11:

> But what things were gain to me, these I have counted loss for Christ. Yet indeed I also count all things loss for the excellence of the knowledge of Christ Jesus my Lord, for whom I have suffered the loss of all things, and count them as rubbish, that I may gain Christ and be found in Him, not having my own righteousness, which is from the law, but that which is through faith in Christ, the righteousness which is from God by faith; that I may know Him and the power of His resurrection, and the fellowship of His sufferings, being conformed to His death, if, by any means, I may attain to the resurrection from the dead.

As I read the apostle's words, I realized that by walking away from everything I had worked for in ministry, I was taking advantage of an opportunity to know Christ better. I was following His Spirit in obedience to His call. When I looked at it from that perspective, the loss did not seem so great anymore. The loss was no longer a loss, per se; it was a seed sown in righteousness that would bring a harvest in the knowledge of Christ. It was painful, but it was worth the price.

What about you? Are you willing to suffer loss in order to fulfill your prophetic calling? Take your time thinking about this, and just follow the leading of the Holy Spirit. He might not be asking you to give up anything right now, but there could come a day when He asks you the same question that He asked me.

How will you respond?

4

No Two Prophets Are Alike

The four of us sat around the table trying to mesh as a prophetic presbytery. We had been charged with walking in Ezra 5—serving as Haggais and Zechariahs to prophesy to apostolic builders in the face of opposition. We were a diverse group. One prophet was nearly sixty years old; the others were much younger. One prophet was white; the others were black. One prophet was from a foreign nation; the others were average Americans. One prophet was well off financially; the others were struggling. One prophet was highly educated; the others were not.

Somehow, we had to figure out how best to use our God-given prophetic giftings to offer edification, exhortation and comfort to the congregation of the church we attended in the midst of spiritual warfare. We needed to get onto the same page. As we gathered around a dining table in a back room of the church, we decided to explore how our prophetic giftings manifested and how we might best complement one another to complete the mission of discerning spiritual attacks against the church, waging war against them and encouraging the saints in the work of building the Church.

After all: "There are diversities of gifts, but the same Spirit. There are differences of ministries, but the same Lord. And there are diversities of activities, but it is the same God who works all in all" (1 Corinthians 12:4–6). Paul used those words as an introduction to the nine gifts of the Spirit. But Paul's words also ring true in the realm of prophetic ministry. You might say: "There are diversities of prophetic gifts, but the same Spirit. There are differences in prophetic ministries, but the same Lord. And there are diversities of prophetic activities, but it is the same God who works all in all the prophets."

Wisdom Does Not Compare (or Copy)

Mentors and role models in prophetic ministry are necessary, but it is important to allow God to develop your unique identity in Christ during the making process. I always like to say, "You can't put a prophet in a box." In other words, there are common characteristics among prophetic giftings, but you cannot stamp, package and label prophets, for no two are exactly alike. We all have different prophetic fingerprints. Prophets typically flow in multiple manifestations of the prophetic anointing, but typically with one area of greatest strength. Some have a stronger call to intercession while others may have a greater bent toward preaching, singing, personal prophecy, writing or some other manifestation of the prophetic gift.

On this prophetic team, I was operating in my primary gifting as the watchman. Since I "see" deception and trouble coming, I was the one on the team who saw the enemy's assignment in the Spirit long before it manifested in the natural. I was the one to blow the trumpet and sound the alarm. I am also a teacher, so I could deliver the message in ways that people could digest. Being a watchman is not a popular position to stand in. Often, it means delivering news people have no desire to hear. But that was my role.

Alice operated in her primary gifting of prophetic intercessor. She would take the watchman information, build a wall of prayer and stand in the gap to bind the enemy's assignment—meaning break, thwart or prevent those evil plans from manifesting (see Ezekiel 22:30). Of course, we all interceded about the issue. All prophets are intercessors. But she had an especially strong prophetic intercession gift that revealed specifics we needed to know in order to combat the enemy.

Evelyn was a strong deliverance minister. She was the one to go in when we needed something rooted out or pulled down. And Billy was a strong prophetic preacher. His sermons would plow through, destroy and throw down the enemy's plans.

Again, God would use us all in different ways from time to time. But we understood our strengths and how we could best flow as a company of prophets in a local church.

We did not compare our prophetic giftings with one another's for the purpose of puffing one up or putting another down. Paul says those who measure themselves by themselves and compare themselves among themselves are not wise (see 2 Corinthians 10:12). Nor did we take on an independent spirit and pretend we did not really need the others to accomplish the mission. We understood Paul's admonishment that there are indeed many members, but one Body (see 1 Corinthians 12:20). The watchman could not say she did not need the intercessor, and the intercessor could not say she had no need for the deliverance minister. We needed to function as a prophetic body, yielding to one another for the greater good. Paul put it this way:

> For as we have many members in one body, but all the members do not have the same function, so we, being many, are one body in Christ, and individually members of one another. Having then gifts differing according to the grace that is given to us, let us use them.
>
> Romans 12:4–6

Prophets have prophetic giftings that differ according to the grace given them. It is up to God to shape your prophetic ministry. In other words, it is not your job to decide how to flow, how to operate in your gifting. It is your job to yield to the Spirit and let Him flow through you as He wills. Trying to be like some other prophet you admire is not God's plan, and could lead you away from His will into performance-oriented ministry at best or into deception at worst.

Think about it for a minute. What if David had tried to be another Moses? What if Elijah had tried to be another Deborah? What if John the Baptist had tried to be another Elisha? They would not have fulfilled their prophetic destinies. Each of these prophets had a unique call of God on his or her life even though, at times, their ministries displayed some similar characteristics.

Fundamentally, prophetic ministry produces reformers, deliverers, intercessors, watchmen, forerunners, singers, musicians, writers, preachers, artists and others who proclaim the will of the Lord. One person's prophetic ministry may look altogether different from another person's prophetic ministry. Thank God, for instance, that John the Baptist stayed focused on his forerunner mission to prepare the way for the Lord instead of trying to work miracles like Elisha. The Bible does not record a single miracle performed by John the Baptist, yet Jesus said that among those born of women there had not risen anyone greater than he (see Matthew 11:11). At the end of this age your rewards will not be based on how flashy your prophetic ministry was. What will matter is the extent to which you were a good and faithful servant with the gifts God gave you.

Distinctions within the Prophetic Gifting

Prophecy is foremost a revelation gift. The purpose of prophecy is to speak out the heart, mind and will of God, bringing edification, exhortation and comfort to the Body of Christ.

Within that larger picture are numerous distinctions of how the gift operates. Again, prophets can be warriors, reformers, deliverers, watchmen, miracle workers, dreamers, visionaries and intercessors—or any combination of these.

All prophets encounter spiritual warfare as a matter of course, and some prophets are particularly equipped in this area. They have a keen sense of discerning of spirits, for instance—they can hear the voice of the demon that is speaking to a person in bondage, see that spirit's manifestation in one's personality or understand how the Holy Spirit wants to move in a service. Or they might have what is known as a "breaker" anointing, meaning that their prayers break through spiritual opposition. Prophets who are called into God's army as spiritual warfare generals in the last days are comparable to Old Testament prophets who were warriors in their time.

David is probably the best-known example of a warrior prophet—he actually led God's army into battle. God told David he was a "man of war" (1 Chronicles 28:3). This is a characteristic of the Lord Himself. Exodus 15:3 says, "The Lord is a man of war; the Lord is His name." Although the prophet David was also a psalmist and a man of prayer—remember that prophets typically flow in multiple manifestations of the prophetic anointing—God made his name great through warfare, beginning with the defeat of Goliath.

Prophetesses can be just as fierce spiritual warriors as their male counterparts. Our Old Testament model is Deborah. Deborah—who happened to be married—was a prophetess and a judge of Israel (see Judges 4:4–5). She had a prophetic word for Barak, the commander of Israel's army, to deploy troops at Mount Tabor against Sisera, the commander of the Canaanite army. The prophecy gave specific instructions to take ten thousand soldiers, and it offered the promise of victory. But Barak did not exactly rise to the occasion: "If you will go with me, then I will go; but if you will not go with me, I will not go!" (Judges 4:8).

This warrior prophetess told Barak she would go with him, but that he would get no glory for the victory. Although Barak led the army, the enemy was delivered into the hands of a woman named Jael who drove a tent peg through Sisera's skull. Deborah was a brave warrior and prophetess, and she demonstrated greater faith than Barak. She goes down in Bible history as a heroine. Some of the most discerning spiritual warriors I have seen in my day have been women with what is often called a "Deborah anointing."

While some prophets are known for flowing in the miraculous, not every prophet is a miracle-worker. Again, we know that John the Baptist did not perform a single miracle (see John 10:41). Elijah, on the other hand, worked plenty of miracles, and Elisha, his protégé, worked twice as many recorded miracles. Another miracle-working prophet, Moses, was used by God to stop and start plagues in Egypt, part the Red Sea and bring water from a rock.

Most true prophets carry a reforming voice. John the Baptist was a reformer—a prophetic messenger who prepared the way for the revelation of Christ. John came on to the public scene baptizing in the wilderness and preaching a baptism of repentance for the remission of sins (see Mark 1:4). "Repent!" is the cry of prophets with a special anointing for reformation. Like Moses, some prophets are deliverers. Demons may even manifest in their presence. Although any believer who understands his authority in Christ can cast out devils in the name of Jesus, some prophets seem to have a stronger anointing, along with the gift of discerning of spirits, to put a dent in the darkness of this world through deliverance ministry.

Ezekiel is an excellent example of a prophet who is called to serve the Kingdom as a watchman (see Ezekiel 3:17). As I mentioned earlier, the watchman ministry is not always popular because the prophet often sees some weapon being formed against a person or church congregation. Many people who hear these warnings accuse the prophets of focusing on the enemy rather than on God. They talk about the importance of edifying the Body and want to receive prophecies of blessing or important ministry callings—not of the fact that there might be devils lurking around.

As you would imagine, the watchman ministry goes hand in hand with intercession. Remember: All prophets are intercessors. Abraham was an intercessor. Moses was an intercessor. Daniel was an intercessor. And Luke mentions an elderly prophetess named Anna "who did not depart from the temple, but served God with fastings and prayers night and day" (Luke 2:37).

Some prophets have grand dreams and visions, like Daniel and Zechariah. Others have a strong teaching gift, like Samuel. And still others are musically gifted, like David. Here is the point: Do not put yourself into a box that you think defines what a prophet should be. Do not try to minister in the same manner as another prophet. Whatever way God has gifted you prophetically, embrace it and be confident in the gift of God working in you.

5

Pursuing Intimacy with God

When I got saved, I looked immediately for any and every opportunity to serve God. I vacuumed floors in the kids' classrooms. I worked behind book tables at church conferences. I stuffed envelopes. I licked stamps. If someone asked me to do it, I did it gladly. There is nothing wrong with that—in fact, a strong desire to serve God should stir in the new believer's heart—but my motives were not completely pure. I did not realize it at the time, but my sincere desire to serve the Lord was overtaken by my zeal to climb a new ladder called *ministry*.

It did not take long for the pastor of that performance-oriented church to notice my drive and put me to work. He gave me a title, authority and various other ministry privileges others envied. Soon enough, I was volunteering as many hours in ministry as I was working in my business. I was essentially holding down two full-time jobs. That left very little time for family, rest, exercise or anything else. My life was falling apart and my health was deteriorating at the expense of the "work of the ministry." Nevertheless, fear of failure drove me to keep "pressing in" until I burned out and had nothing left to give anyone.

Something had shifted. Instead of serving the Lord, I had begun performing for the approval of man. Although I truly did have a heart to serve God, I was seeking the Father's approval through man's affirmation. I learned the hard way that God will never push us further than He gives us the grace to go—but people will. And because I found my self-worth in what I could do for God rather than in what He had already done for me—because I was not rooted in the revelation of who I am in Christ and how much God the Father loves me—I was consumed by religious works at the expense of intimacy with the One who had prepared the good works for me to walk in (see Ephesians 2:10). The result, again, was physical and spiritual burnout.

When the Holy Spirit moved me on to a healthier church, I entered into a season of rest. At first it was almost painful not to serve in ministry. I felt as though I was going stir crazy just sitting in the congregation week after week. But as I sat and received—as I allowed my soul to drink in the messages of the Father's love that were coming through the worship team and the preachers—I found the missing link in the chain that would allow me to serve God out of a pure heart of love rather than a need for approval, recognition or success. I received a revelation of the Father's heart and developed greater intimacy with God that has served me well in prophetic ministry.

Jesus: An Expression of the Father's Heart

Jesus spent three years in ministry on earth, in part, to reveal the personality of the Father. When Jesus was raising the dead, healing the sick, cleansing the lepers, feeding the masses, providing finances, befriending sinners, extending forgiveness, teaching the Word and working various other miracles, He was mirroring the kind intentions of His Father's heart toward us.

You probably have no problem believing that Jesus is a kind, brotherly Messiah who saved us from our sins and continually makes intercession for us in heaven. But too many believers have a false impression about Father God. Too many believe the Father is stern and hard—and just waiting for an opportunity to sideline us or even banish us from the Kingdom. This harsh concept of God the Father is damaging to your soul—and your prophetic ministry—because you could wind up prophesying with a hard edge that pushes people away from God rather than compelling them to run to Him. Prophets need to speak the truth—even the hardest truths—in love. That can be difficult to do without a revelation of the Father's heart.

So what does the Father heart of God look like? Jesus told Thomas that anyone who has seen Him has seen the Father (see John 14:5–9). In other words, it is in the Father's heart to raise the dead, heal the sick, cleanse the lepers, feed the masses, provide finances, befriend sinners, extend forgiveness, teach the Word and work various other miracles. God the Father does not love you any less than Jesus loves you. In fact, He loves you just as He loves Jesus (see John 17:23). Meditate on that. It is a powerful truth that will propel you into greater intimacy with God.

Without intimacy with God, you cannot fulfill His perfect plan for your life no matter what you are called to do. Intimacy with God strengthens your spirit. Intimacy with God refreshes the weary soul. Intimacy with God protects you from temptation. Intimacy with God anchors your emotions. Intimacy with God builds trust. Intimacy with God is fundamental and vital for every believer, but consider how vital it is for the prophet whom God wants to entrust with the secrets of His heart, the prophetic messenger who speaks forth His thoughts. Think about it for a minute. We share the secrets of our hearts with close friends or family—people with whom we are in intimate relationship, people we can trust. Does it not follow that God would do the same?

Developing Intimacy

God wants to develop an intimate relationship with you that mirrors the intimate relationship He had with Jesus while He walked the earth. Jesus did only what He saw His Father do. Indeed, Jesus and the Father were in such close relationship that Jesus would not take a single step without Him. This was both a sign of the intimacy Jesus had with His Father and the humility that marked the Son of God. Jesus said:

> I assure you, most solemnly I tell you, the Son is able to do nothing of Himself (of His own accord); but He is able to do only what He sees the Father doing, for whatever the Father does is what the Son does in the same way [in His turn]. The Father dearly loves the Son and discloses to (shows) Him everything that He Himself does. And He will disclose to Him (let Him see) greater things yet than these, so that you may marvel and be full of wonder and astonishment.
>
> John 5:19–20 AMPLIFIED

Jesus also said,

> I am able to do nothing from Myself [independently, of My own accord—but only as I am taught by God and as I get His orders]. Even as I hear, I judge [I decide as I am bidden to decide. As the voice comes to Me, so I give a decision], and My judgment is right (just, righteous), because I do not seek or consult My own will [I have no desire to do what is pleasing to Myself, My own aim, My own purpose] but only the will and pleasure of the Father Who sent Me.
>
> John 5:30 AMPLIFIED

In these verses, Jesus explained that He saw and heard prophetically what the Father wanted Him to do. Obedience rose naturally out of intimacy.

Mature prophetic ministry flows from this level of intimacy with and obedience to God. When we receive Jesus as our Savior, we are not only saved from the kingdom of darkness—we are also saved into close fellowship with God. Jesus prayed: "This is eternal life, that they may know You, the only true God, and Jesus Christ whom You have sent" (John 17:3).

Without understanding God's love—without knowing in your heart that God loves you for who you are and not for what you do—you will never develop fully in your prophetic gifting. You run the risk of prophesying out of a wrong spirit if you are not rooted and grounded in the love of Christ. I believe you can develop in your prophetic calling only to the degree to which you understand His love for you and for mankind.

Maturing in Love

If you are born again, you have received the Spirit of adoption by whom we cry, "Abba, Father" (see Romans 8:15). The Aramaic word *abba* is the word we use today for *papa*. Like Jesus, Paul painted the Father as a caring, loving Dad who is concerned about every area of your life. The Father cares so much about you that He even knows how many hairs are on your head (see Luke 12:7). He loves you so much that He collects your tears in a bottle and records all your sorrows in a book (see Psalm 56:8).

John was marveling at the Father's heart when he wrote: "Behold what manner of love the Father has bestowed on us, that we should be called children of God!" (1 John 3:1). God "demonstrates His own love toward us, in that while we were still sinners, Christ died for us" (Romans 5:8). And again, God actually loves us just as much as He loves Jesus! (see John 17:23). He loved us before we loved Him (see 1 John 4:19). And He loves us with an everlasting love (see Jeremiah 31:3).

Love is the motive behind all true prophecy. Remember, the purpose of prophecy is to reveal the heart, mind and will of God.

Without intimacy with Father, Son and Holy Spirit, you cannot prophesy what is on His heart with consistent accuracy. And if prophecy is not coming from the heart of our loving God—and if it is not delivered in that spirit of love, even when giving a call to repentance—then it is best left unspoken because it is not truly representing God. We are always supposed to speak the truth in love (see Ephesians 4:15).

God can and does speak through young or immature prophets. He uses the pure-hearted where they are as they grow in love and walk with Him through the making process. But the Holy Spirit's ultimate goal is to raise up mature prophets who see and hear what the Father is doing and saying, and act according to His will. Cultivating intimacy with the Father is part and parcel of the making process.

Rather than pursuing spiritual gifts, speaking invitations or other ministry opportunities, seek first the heart of the Father to discover who He really is, what His personality is like and His ways of leading and guiding. David prayed, "Show me Your ways, O Lord; teach me Your paths. Lead me in Your truth and teach me, for You are the God of my salvation; on You I wait all the day" (Psalm 25:4–5). When you connect with God's heart with pure motives, He will give you everything your heart desires (see Psalm 37:4).

6

Melt Me, Mold Me, Fill Me, Use Me

"Oh, God, break us! Break us, God!" That was the impassioned cry on the lips of one brave soul on our prophetic team meeting many years ago. I could not believe I was hearing him lift up such a dangerous prayer! I had been warned over the years never to pray for patience because such petitions typically lead to trials. I could not imagine what a prayer for "breaking" would lead to.

To be sure, his Spirit-inspired prayer terrified me because I had read about how God embarrasses prophets publicly—and repeatedly—in order to teach them humility, holiness and obedience. Yet, despite my soulish horror, I found my spirit agreeing with the "breaking" prayer. Still, after I left that meeting I was scared about what was going to happen next. After all, what young prophetic messenger has not read these words in John and Paula Sandford's classic *The Elijah Task*:

> What discipline, training and chastisement is required! The prophet, more than all others, save the apostle, must die to self, daily. His word must not be his own. What dire warnings

Jeremiah 23 and Ezekiel 13 heap upon the soulish prophet who speaks not out of God's Spirit but from the contrary winds of his own soul. No beginner can be that pure. God teaches in the rude world of trial and error. Therefore the budding prophet will be thrashed, beaten, humiliated, scorned, laughed at, and rejected, will fall into error and arise—only to fall again, until, in every part of him, like Nebuchadnezzar, he knows with grass in his mouth that the "Most High rules the kingdom of men and gives it to whom he will" (Daniel 4:32).

The Fear of Being Broken

Does this mean we enter prophetic ministry with fearful imaginations about what might happen to us during the breaking process? Not at all. Our eyes should not be on a rude world of trial and error, along with thrashings, beatings, humiliation, scorn, ridicule, rejection and falling into error. Rather, Paul gave us our direction when he exhorted the Philippians:

> Whatever things are true, whatever things are noble, whatever things are just, whatever things are pure, whatever things are lovely, whatever things are of good report, if there is any virtue and if there is anything praiseworthy—meditate on these things.
>
> Philippians 4:8

If you launch into prophetic ministry with fear in your heart, you are likely to resist the breaking and be marred in the hand of the Potter. If that happens, you could miss your highest calling in the prophetic. Rather than fear God's training process, we should fear missing His best for us

Consider this Scripture: "I went down to the potter's house, and there he was, making something at the wheel. And the vessel that he made of clay was marred in the hand of the potter; so he made it again into another vessel, as it seemed good to the potter to make" (Jeremiah 18:3–4). *The Message* puts verse 4 this way: "Whenever the pot the potter was working on turned out badly, as sometimes happens when you are working with clay, the potter would simply start over and use the same clay to make another pot."

Look at it like this: You are the lump of clay and God is the Potter. God is actively molding you to fulfill your prophetic destiny. He is molding you into a vessel of honor, but you have a part to play in the molding. Paul explained it this way:

> But in a great house there are not only vessels of gold and silver, but also [utensils] of wood and earthenware, and some for honorable and noble [use] and some for menial and ignoble [use]. So whoever cleanses himself [from what is ignoble and unclean, who separates himself from contact with contaminating and corrupting influences] will [then himself] be a vessel set apart and useful for honorable and noble purposes, consecrated and profitable to the Master, fit and ready for any good work.
>
> 2 Timothy 2:20–21 AMPLIFIED

Again, God is actively molding you to fulfill your prophetic destiny. He is molding you into a vessel of honor, but you have a part to play. Your part is to yield to the Potter's hand. Your part is to shun contaminating and corrupting influences. If you resist God—if you are stiff-necked, stubborn, rebellious or otherwise uncooperative—you could end up a vessel of dishonor instead of an honorable mouthpiece of God. You could end up marred in the hand of the Potter. God might mold you into a different shape, but you would never reach your highest prophetic calling.

God's breaking process is nothing to fear. God is a good and loving God, and He has a perfect plan for your life. Granted, it is not fun to encounter the discipline of God or to walk through fire or give up something dear to you, but when you keep in mind the things above (see Colossians 3:2), you can embrace the process and rejoice in the breaking. As Paul said: "No chastening seems to be joyful for the present, but painful; nevertheless, afterward it yields the peaceable fruit of righteousness to those who have been trained by it" (Hebrews 12:11).

The Purpose of the Breaking Process

Understanding the purpose of the breaking process can help alleviate the fear that often accompanies images of thrashings, beatings, humiliation, scorn, ridicule, rejection and falling into error. So what is the purpose?

As the name suggests, God's breaking process intends to "break off" those character qualities that are not godly in order to create a humbler, more honorable vessel—one that is willing and obedient. The breaking process works to train prophets to walk in the Spirit, sow to the Spirit (see Galatians 6:8) and otherwise manifest the fruit of the Spirit. If you cooperate with the Holy Spirit, you will eventually emerge as a statesman for the Kingdom of God with the credibility and character you need to deliver a pure word of the Lord.

The late Kathryn Kuhlman used to sing a song at her meetings called "Spirit of the Living God." The lyrics went: "Spirit of the Living God, fall afresh on me! . . . Melt me, mold me, fill me, use me." This should be the cry of the prophet. Yield to the Spirit of God as He moves to shape your character, rooting out issues that keep the prophetic anointing from flowing freely. Resisting God never turns out well. Yielding to the hand of the Potter, pursuing intimate relationship with the Father no matter how He is moving in your life might be uncomfortable, but you will maintain peace.

This brings us to the question of what you can expect—and how you should respond—during this making process. Will you really be thrashed, beaten, humiliated, scorned, ridiculed, rejected and prone to falling into error?

What to Expect in the Making

When I was pregnant with my daughter, I purchased a book called *What to Expect When You Are Expecting*. As the title suggests, the book laid out what to expect during my pregnancy, week by week. I found it to be accurate at times and completely inaccurate at other times. Sometimes, what I read scared me—and it never happened. And sometimes, I experienced issues that were not in the book!

To be sure, no two prophets are on the same path. That means there is not a detailed checklist I can give outlining the specific details of your individual making process. But James did offer some insight into the life of a prophetic messenger. James 5:10 says: "My brethren, take the prophets, who spoke in the name of the Lord, as an example of suffering and patience." *The Message* puts it this way: "Take the old prophets as your mentors. They put up with anything, went through everything, and never once quit, all the time honoring God."

So what can you expect during the breaking process? Simply put, whatever it takes to mold you into a prophetic vessel of honor suitable for the Master's use. My character flaws are different from yours. Your strengths are different from mine. But broadly speaking, you can expect to suffer and you can expect to learn patience during the making process. Only after you have died to contaminating and corrupting influences and developed the godly character traits you are lacking can God trust you to be His spokesman on the largest platforms.

You might need to die to a pursuit of recognition and develop your faith. You might need to die to pride and develop the virtue of humility. You might need to die to a know-it-all attitude and develop true biblical knowledge. You might need to die to lust and develop self-control. You might need to die to a quitter's attitude and develop perseverance. You might need to die to unholy habits and develop godly ones. You might need to die to a sharp tongue and develop kindness. Or you might need to die to selfishness and learn to walk in love. Peter put it this way:

> But also for this very reason, giving all diligence, add to your faith virtue, to virtue knowledge, to knowledge self-control, to self-control perseverance, to perseverance godliness, to godliness brotherly kindness, and to brotherly kindness love. For if these things are yours and abound, you will be neither barren nor unfruitful in the knowledge of our Lord Jesus Christ. For he who lacks these things is shortsighted, even to blindness, and has forgotten that he was cleansed from his old sins. Therefore, brethren, be even more diligent to make your call and election sure, for if you do these things you will never stumble.
>
> 2 Peter 1:5–10

What a promise!

Your Customized Wilderness Place

God does not want you to stumble—especially not on a ministry platform where people could be hurt and disillusioned by your missteps. For that reason, God creates a customized wilderness just for you. In this wilderness you can stumble and fall until you are strong enough in your prophetic walk—and skilled enough in spiritual warfare—to carry your mantle with integrity.

Don't get me wrong. That does not mean that God will not use you during the breaking process. He began using me in my local church almost immediately after He called me. But He also used experiences there, for better or worse, to train me. It was years before He put me on an international platform of influence, and even when He did, it took years longer to gain credibility in prophetic ministry. That is the way it should be. So, yes, God will use you right after He calls you. But you will not reach your highest calling until you have been battle tested and God knows that He can trust you. That means going through the wilderness—and often more than once.

I went through the wilderness wanting a title and recognition; I came out of the wilderness wanting only to fulfill my divine commission, even if no one recognized me and no matter what people called me. I went into the wilderness wanting admiration from those around me; I came out of the wilderness wanting to see Him admired by the world. I used to teach the party line— what I was taught—like a parrot; now I teach what the Holy Spirit tells me to teach whether anyone likes it or not. Through the breaking, my prophetic ministry has become an expression of what God has delivered me from, what He has done in me and what He is impressing upon my heart.

When you go through the wilderness, you understand that prophetic ministry is not about theology alone; it is also about experience. You learn the truth of the Word practically through personal experiences—and you walk out that truth before ever preaching it. See, God has to take you through something before you can share it without a judgmental spirit. Going through trials and tribulations helps you learn to trust God rather than man. And that helps keep your prophetic message pure.

Paul explained it this way:

We have this treasure in earthen vessels, that the excellence of the power may be of God and not of us. We are hard-pressed on every side, yet not crushed; we are perplexed, but not in despair; persecuted, but not forsaken; struck down, but not destroyed— always carrying about in the body the dying of the Lord Jesus, that the life of Jesus also may be manifested in our body. For we who live are always delivered to death for Jesus' sake, that the life of Jesus also may be manifested in our mortal flesh. So then death is working in us, but life in you.

2 Corinthians 4:7–12

Remember, the making process never ends. You will always be dying to something. You will always be gaining a deeper revelation of who God is and how He moves. As this process continues, more of Christ's life will shine through you. Your prophetic ministry will become increasingly accurate and more powerful. So decide in your heart right now not to fear the breaking—embrace it. It helps make you.

7

Facing Down the Tempter

Every prophet will have to face down the tempter more than once—and, in fact, probably many, many times—whether traversing a wilderness place or serving in active ministry. The enemy is quite aware that one impure prophet can bring reproach upon the entire prophetic ministry—and some already have. Peter warns us to be vigilant, because our "adversary the devil walks about like a roaring lion, seeking whom he may devour" (1 Peter 5:8). The enemy delights in discrediting God's mouthpieces. He will show up at opportune times to sabotage your ministry. At different points along the road to prophetic maturity, you will be enticed and tempted to do wrong. You will need to stand strong if you are going to grow to maturity and be ready for the Potter's use.

Satan has many names—the evil one, the father of lies, the accuser of the brethren. These are all aspects of his wicked character. But one of his names—the tempter—describes the allure of sin in the prophet's life. If the tempter could woo the prophet David, a man after God's own heart, then no prophet is immune.

The tempter uses what is in us, of course. We will discuss in the next chapter the youthful lusts that Paul told Timothy to flee, as well as the carnal lusts that plague every believer. Also, let's not discuss sexual sin here; we will explore that topic in chapter 17. Rather, let's look at the subtler temptations he uses that tap in to soulish insecurities or impatience, especially when you are in a wilderness place.

You might be tempted to prove your prophetic calling to the world. Giving in to this is a sign of immaturity that will hold you back from the fullness of the prophetic anointing. You might face the temptation to pursue the wrong kind of power or idolize the wrong god—or even to accept the worship and adoration of those who follow your ministry. It is fine to receive sincere compliments, but you should always point to Jesus as the One you serve. Taking credit that belongs to Him will lead you to a fall. You might also face a temptation to misuse the Word—or take it out of context—for personal gain or to prove a point. That will lead you into serious error.

Indeed, these are the very strategies the tempter used against Jesus when He was in the wilderness. Jesus, of course, showed us the way to overcome each of these temptations: staying grounded in the written Word of God. You have probably heard it said that Satan does not have any new tricks. Well, he does not have any new temptations, either. They all have to do with "the lust of the flesh, the lust of the eyes, and the pride of life"—all that is in the world (1 John 2:16).

Put another way, temptations succeed when you want your own way, want everything for yourself and want to appear important. This opens the door wide to the tempter. I believe that if you can see the tempter, you can defeat him. If you think you are beyond temptation—in any area—the devil might use your prideful stance to set you up for a fall. When you rely on the Word of God as your guide, you will not fail. The Word of God "is sharper than any two-edged sword, piercing even to the division of soul and spirit, and of joints and marrow, and is a discerner of the thoughts and intents of the heart" (Hebrews 4:12).

Tempted to Prove Your Prophetic Gift

Let's look at the temptation of Jesus in the wilderness to see how the devil often works—and how to respond. Jesus was full of the Holy Spirit. (How about you? Without the Holy Spirit's help, we will never thwart the tempter.) After Jesus was baptized, He was led by the Holy Spirit into the wilderness, where the devil tempted Him for forty days (see Luke 4:1–2).

At the end of His forty-day fast—nearly six weeks—when Jesus was hungry, the tempter continued his assault with three temptations that are recorded in Scripture.

First, the devil said to Jesus: "If You are the Son of God, command this stone to become bread" (Luke 4:3). Notice the enemy's strategy. He typically comes to tempt us when we are in a vulnerable position. Maybe it is during a season of prayer and fasting. Maybe it is during a time of intense spiritual warfare. Maybe it is during a life transition. Temptations during those times often come with a provoking spirit. That was the enemy's strategy against Jesus. The devil waited until Jesus was hungry and then tried to provoke Him, saying, "If You are the Son of God, turn this stone into bread." The key word here is *if*.

It was almost as if the devil was saying, "Prove Your identity by using Your power—I dare You!" The devil knew full well who Jesus was, and he knows who you are in Christ. The devil also knows that you have the authority in Jesus' name to bind—to thwart or stop—his wicked operations. You do not have anything to prove to the devil or to anyone else. You need only to obey God from a pure heart.

Remember that the next time the devil tempts you to prophesy in order to demonstrate your gift—to prove your identity—in the local church or on a speaking circuit. You might be tempted to prophesy despite the absence of an unction from the Holy Spirit, which can harm the saints who hear it and the Church Body as a whole. Sometimes young prophets compete for the spotlight, each hoping to be the one to give the most astounding or most accurate prophetic word. This motivation is always a mistake and can lead to serious error.

Has the tempter ever challenged your calling into prophetic ministry? I know he has challenged mine, especially in the early years. Have you ever felt the need to prove the authenticity of your prophetic gift? Been tempted to offer some sign that you are called into prophetic ministry? Hoped people would call you by a title? I struggled with that in the beginning. But Jesus showed me clearly that He is not interested in offering complementary signs for validation and does not care about titles. He is not concerned about proving Himself. Nor is He planning to show off in order to appease my ego. Never let the devil provoke you into misusing or mistiming your prophetic gift.

Provocation aside, this temptation sought to entice Jesus to use His power for personal provision. Specifically, the devil tempted a hungry man to perform a miracle to satisfy the flesh. This is a keen strategy against prophets. The enemy tempts prophets to use the gifts of the Spirit to meet their personal needs rather than the needs of others—for they should be trusting God to meet their own personal needs. Prophets who fall for this temptation often sell (made-up) prophetic words, anointing oils and prayer shawls for big bucks to saints deceived by glitz or even by a false anointing.

Jesus taught us how to respond to such temptations—speak and obey the Word. Jesus answered Satan's provocation by quoting Deuteronomy: "It is written, 'Man shall not live by bread alone, but by every word of God'" (Luke 4:4). In other words, trust God's Word. He is the One who called you into prophetic ministry, and He will reveal that calling to other people when it suits Him. He is also the One who supplies all of your needs according to His riches in glory by Christ Jesus (see Philippians 4:19). Never give in to the temptation to prove who you are or to use your gifts for personal gain. Those motives will lead you out of God's will, which is a dangerous place to be.

Tempted to Seek Fame, Glamour and Riches

Next, the devil led Jesus up to a high place and showed Him all the kingdoms of the world. It is interesting that Jesus followed the devil to this high place. He did not have to go, but He submitted Himself to the temptation. (Yes, it was a temptation or the Bible would not have called it a temptation.) I believe He went to show us the way out.

Jesus wanted us to be aware of one of the devil's most successful tricks: the offer of worldly fame, glamour and riches in exchange for our worship. Satan is the god of this world and many are worshiping him (or at least his worldly idols) whether they know it or not (see 2 Corinthians 4:4). Sadly, even some God-ordained prophets are worshiping these glamorous idols rather than pursuing righteousness, faith, love and peace.

In this second temptation, the devil promised to give Jesus authority and splendor if He would worship him (see Luke 4:5). Bowing down to the tempter would have meant that Jesus could have skipped the cross and gone straight to glory—worldly glory, that is. Prophets who bow down to the tempter might skirt the making process and find worldly glory, but it will not last in the age to come and often does not even last through this age. When prophets fall, it is usually because they got ahead of God's timing in the face of opportunity for fame, glamour or riches.

Guard yourself from temptations like "the cares and anxieties of the world and distractions of the age, and the pleasure and delight and false glamour and deceitfulness of riches, and the craving and passionate desire for other things [that] creep

in and choke and suffocate the Word" (Mark 4:19 Amplified).
If you fall to these temptations, your life and ministry will bear
the wrong kind of fruit. And, ultimately, your fruit will expose
your heart.

When the tempter comes with these tactics—and he will—
respond as Jesus did. Jesus once again refused the temptation, combating it with the Word: "Worship the Lord your
God and only the Lord your God. Serve him with absolute
single-heartedness" (Luke 4:8 Message). Serving the Lord with
single-heartedness in pursuit of righteousness will help you
maintain a pure and vibrant spirit that recognizes and flees this
temptation.

Tempted to Violate Scripture

When the tempter failed with these tactics, he took the spiritual warfare to a whole new level. The devil actually sought
to kill Jesus by tempting Him to apply the Word of God in
the wrong way. The tempter took Jesus to Jerusalem and had
Him stand on the highest point of the Temple, saying, "If you
are God's Son, jump. It's written, isn't it, that 'he has placed
you in the care of angels to protect you; they will catch you;
you won't so much as stub your toe on a stone'?" (Luke 4:9–11
Message).

See, the devil finally caught on to Jesus' strategy of using
the written Word to counter his temptations and adjusted his
tactics midstream, using the Word itself against his foe. If the
devil could have provoked Jesus to jump, the Son of God would
have aborted His calling. He would have left the prophetic words
of many prophets unfulfilled—and violated Scripture on more
than one level. Again, the devil was attacking Jesus' identity
with this temptation—"*If* You are the Son of God."

Be careful that you rightly divide the Word of Truth. Remember, the tempter knows the Word of God inside and out.

After all, he has had a lot longer to study it than you have. The devil will misuse Scripture in order to deceive you. He will also try to cause you to misuse Scripture for your own benefit or to prove a point in your preaching. The thought will be subtle, and it might even seem right to you at the time. It could sound like revelation—and it might be. But it might also come from a spirit of error.

I think that this temptation, the temptation to misuse the Word of God, is many times successful because prophets are under far too much pressure to prophesy in today's Church. Prophets are under great stress to prove their identity as prophets, to raise offerings or to respond to world events with deep prophetic insight.

The frequency of prophetic words is not and should not be the only measure of a true prophet, nor is the depth of revelation. Most of Jesus' revelations were simple, yet profound. Further, the enemy may tempt you to use the Word of God out of context to support a prophetic word or some other deep revelation you think you have discovered in Scripture. The tempter's ultimate goal in all of this is to get you to move beyond the Holy Spirit and beyond the Word of God so he can lead you into error. Keep the Word in its context: the context of the passage, the chapter, the book and the whole canon of Scripture.

Traps of the Enemy

Remember not to think too highly of yourself. Anyone can fall into these temptations. Yes, we are more than conquerors in Christ Jesus, but even Superman had to deal with kryptonite. Our kryptonite is called temptation. Watch for

the temptation to prove your prophetic gift
the temptation to obtain worldly fame, glamour and riches
the temptation to manipulate the Word of God

These are traps of the enemy—trying to prove you are a prophet, trying to profit from your gift or trying to have your own way. When the tempter comes, rise up in the Spirit, tell the devil who you really are in Christ and what the Word says.

Remember, it is written in James 4:7: "Submit to God. Resist the devil and he will flee from you."

8

Passion for Holiness

When I was in college, I dreamed of becoming a film editor. I read books on filmmaking. I studied the greats. I attended seminars. I spent weekends making documentaries with a Super 8 camera and wrote screenplays during the week. Of course, all the subjects were worldly. I did not know any better; I was not saved.

After I got saved, I stopped going to the movies—except for children's films with my then-young daughter. So when a friend suggested having movie night in my living room, I thought it would be a fun time. After all, she was a Spirit-filled Christian and a teacher in our church. I figured she would bring some old classic film or a new Christian movie—or at least something uplifting and clean. When I saw the title of the DVD she had brought, I really did not want to watch it, but I hated confrontation so we began watching it.

The main character in the movie had issues with God. He was offered supernatural powers and an opportunity to rule the world. The movie contained nudity, sex scenes, violence and filthy language. About halfway through the film, I started actually getting sick to my stomach. It was not solely a physical thing; my spirit was grieved. I finally had to tell my friend that I could not continue watching the movie. She got angry with me, called me "self-righteous" and left.

It was not self-righteousness though. It is not my place to judge others for what they choose to watch or how they choose to live. But the Holy Spirit does not want me watching that sort of content—and He has made this abundantly clear. I have had similar sick-to-my-stomach feelings in other situations—situations that might not bother other Christians who sincerely love Jesus. But a call to prophetic ministry demands *passion* for holiness. It does not mean you never miss the mark. You will miss it. But if you have passion for holiness, you will get back up and continue pursuing God.

I am reminded of the Scripture in which Jesus said this:

> "That servant who knew his master's will, and did not prepare himself or do according to his will, shall be beaten with many stripes. But he who did not know, yet committed things deserving of stripes, shall be beaten with few. For everyone to whom much is given, from him much will be required; and to whom much has been committed, of him they will ask the more."
>
> Luke 12:47–49

Remember that when you answer the call to prophetic ministry, it means submitting to a making process. During that making process the Lord is investing in your development and giving you an opportunity to serve as His mouthpiece. That is a tremendous honor and an awe-inspiring responsibility. God will ask more of you than He asks of many others in the Body of Christ. Staying pure means following a narrower path. Staying pure means cultivating passion for holiness.

Be Holy Even As He Is Holy

When the Lord called me into prophetic ministry, His Spirit offered plenty of wise counsel in line with His written Word.

One of the nuggets of advice He expressly offered was this: *Put aside childish things. I have need of your voice.* "Putting aside childish things" covers a broad spectrum of immature pursuits—leanings that Paul called "youthful lusts."

Indeed, yielding to the Potter means fleeing from our youthful lusts and "[pursuing] righteousness, faith, love, peace with those who call on the Lord out of a pure heart" (2 Timothy 2:22). James asked a pointed question in this regard: "Does a spring send forth fresh water and bitter from the same opening?" (James 3:11–12). *The Message* puts it this way: "A spring doesn't gush fresh water one day and brackish the next, does it?" If we are walking purposely in sin, we are not walking in obedience. It is impossible to pursue holiness and lust at the same time.

A double-minded man is unstable in all his ways (see James 1:8), and God is not in the business of releasing unstable prophets to speak to the nations what is on His heart. Sure, some prophetic messengers may rush out ahead of God's timing with prophetic words that win the attention of the Church—but that does not mean that God is the author of those utterances.

The Message gives us this apt description:

> In a well-furnished kitchen there are not only crystal goblets and silver platters, but waste cans and compost buckets—some containers used to serve fine meals, others to take out the garbage. Become the kind of container God can use to present any and every kind of gift to his guests for their blessing.
>
> 2 Timothy 2:20–21

Sadly, what comes out of some prophets' mouths is comparable to the content of waste cans and compost buckets: It stinks!

I liken what the New King James Version calls "vessels of dishonor" to false prophets who follow after lusts rather than pursuing passion for holiness. But let's concentrate on the prophets of honor that have been sanctified and are worthy of the Master's use. Prophets of honor have not only fled youthful lusts, they have also taken up Paul's advice to pursue righteousness, faith, love and peace.

Run wholeheartedly toward holiness with a healthy fear of the Lord. Cultivate passion to be holy just as He is holy (see 1 Peter 1:16). God is pure from defilement of any kind, and He wants the ones who will speak forth His will to seek that same purity. This is true freedom. More than 150 years ago, British revivalist Henry Varley said: "The world has yet to see what God can do with and for and through a man who is fully and wholly consecrated to Him." Could that person be you?

If no one will see the Lord without pursuing holiness (see Hebrews 12:14), then how can prophets hear and speak for God without pursuing this character trait? True joy—and true effectiveness in prophetic ministry—comes when you understand that you are free from the power of sin, and when you allow the Gospel to purify the way you think, speak and act. True power comes from realizing that He has already made you holy, and deciding by your will and reliance on God's grace to walk it out.

Charles Spurgeon once said:

> If Christ has died for me—ungodly as I am, without strength as I am—then I can no longer live in sin, but must arouse myself to love and serve Him who has redeemed me. I cannot trifle with the evil that killed my best Friend. I must be holy for His sake. How can I live in sin when He has died to save me from it?

Amen.

Declaring War on Carnal Lusts

If you have entered into prophetic ministry, then you have probably figured out by practical experience that you are in a spiritual war against principalities, powers, rulers of the darkness of this world and spiritual wickedness in high places that want to destroy you. But have you ever considered that in your passion for holiness it is not enough to flee youthful lusts? You must also wage spiritual war against carnal lusts within you.

Carnal lusts include more than sexual sin. *Vine's Expository Dictionary* defines this kind of *lust* as a "strong desire" of any kind. Although the Bible uses *lust* in a positive context three times, the Word of God most often describes it as a root of sin. Carnal lust is associated with pride, greed and other strong behaviors that lead us out of God's will.

> Let no one say when he is tempted, "I am tempted by God"; for God cannot be tempted by evil, nor does He Himself tempt anyone. But each one is tempted when he is drawn away by his own desires and enticed. Then, when desire has conceived, it gives birth to sin; and sin, when it is full-grown, brings forth death.
>
> James 1:13–15

When Paul said we do not wrestle against flesh and blood (see Ephesians 6:12), he did not mean that we do not wrestle against fleshly temptations. Indeed, we know that carnal lusts war against our souls (see 1 Peter 2:11). You have to engage in this battle in order to walk out the victory we already have in Christ. You have to declare war on carnal lusts or you might wind up buffeting the air in the name of Jesus while the enemy has his wicked way in your life.

We must wage war on carnal lusts because these strong desires ultimately bring forth death. Paul understood this all too well. Paul not only wrestled the "beasts at Ephesus" (1 Corinthians 15:32), he also wrestled his own carnal desires. He shared his heart in the book of Romans. He knew the right thing to do, but the power of sin kept sabotaging his best intentions. He had the desire to do what was right, but the inability to follow through. He would decide not to do wrong, then do wrong anyway. Sound familiar? Listen in to Paul's confession:

> Something has gone wrong deep within me and gets the better of me every time. It happens so regularly that it's predictable. The moment I decide to do good, sin is there to trip me up. I truly delight in God's commands, but it's pretty obvious that not all of me joins in that delight. Parts of me covertly rebel, and just when I least expect it, they take charge. I've tried everything and nothing helps. I'm at the end of my rope. Is there no one who can do anything for me? Isn't that the real question?
>
> Romans 7:20–24 MESSAGE

That is the real question. But thanks be to God who always causes us to triumph in Christ (see 2 Corinthians 2:14). Jesus Christ acted to set things right in a life of contradictions in which Paul wanted to serve God with all his heart and mind, but was tempted by his carnal nature. Christ is our secret weapon in the war against carnal lusts, too. Paul exhorts us to "put on the Lord Jesus Christ, and make no provision for the flesh, to fulfill its lusts" (Romans 13:12–14).

Pursuing Holy Passion

The best way to pursue holy passion is to keep the lights on. Light shines in darkness and the darkness can never extinguish it. Think about it for a minute. What would happen if you walked into a pitch-black room and tried to find your Bible? You would have to take slow baby steps. Even if a glimmer of light slipped into the room, it would take you a long time to find your Bible because your eyes would have to adjust to darkness. You would probably run into a wall and walk away with a nice bump on your forehead. But if you walked into the room and turned the light on, you would be able to find your Bible quickly.

When it comes to pursuing holiness, that example works out like this: If you focus on all your impurities, shortcomings and sins—if you adjust your eyes to the darkness—you will take baby steps toward freedom and keep hitting the wall. Likewise, when you turn on the light—when you keep your eyes on Jesus—you will find yourself being transformed into His image. When you focus on Jesus, the beauty of His holiness and His love for you, you find the strength to overcome dark temptations of all sorts, from lying to bitterness to pride to greed to immorality.

Light overcomes darkness every time. Where light increases, darkness decreases. So focus on the light. A strong pursuit of God is a recipe for resisting lusts of the flesh. If your eyes are on Him and you connect with Him at a heart level, you will not even want to look at what the enemy is dangling before your eyes or listen to his wicked whispers. When you become lovesick for God, you will have no desire to pursue the passing pleasures of sin. John Piper once said: "Sin is what we do when our hearts are not satisfied with God. God is most glorified in us when we are most satisfied with Him."

It is a mindset shift. Paul put it this way:

> Likewise you also, reckon yourselves to be dead indeed to sin, but alive to God in Christ Jesus our Lord. Therefore do not let sin reign in your mortal body, that you should obey it in its lusts. And do not present your members as instruments of unrighteousness to sin, but present yourselves to God as being alive from the dead, and your members as instruments of righteousness to God.
>
> Romans 6:11–13

You are dead to sin. Keep reminding yourself of that. You are alive to God in Christ. Christ lives in you. Meditate on who you are in Christ. The Holy Spirit dwells in you. You are endued with power to overcome all the power of the enemy. Act as if you believe it. See the light. This revelation of who you are in Christ is more important than any class on prophecy you can take. If you know who Christ is—and you know who you are in Him—you will be able to discern between the true and the false and your prophetic utterances will be more accurate.

Submit Yourself Fully to God

Passion for holiness means holding nothing back. You cannot hold on to your favorite pet sin and still insist you have passion for holiness. I am not talking about the character flaws the Holy Spirit works with us to overcome, one by one, over the course of our lifetimes. We will never be perfect so long as we are in these fleshly bodies. I am talking about knowingly holding on to sin—and even justifying it.

During the making process, God will teach you how to walk by the principles of the Spirit so that you will not fulfill the lust of the flesh (see Galatians 5:16). It is your job to cooperate with His grace. How do you know when you are walking by the principles of the Spirit? Examine the fruit. The works of the flesh are "adultery, fornication, uncleanness, lewdness, idolatry, sorcery, hatred, contentions, jealousies, outbursts of wrath, selfish ambitions, dissensions, heresies, envy, murder, drunkenness, revelries, and the like" (Galatians 5:19–21). By contrast, the fruit of the Spirit is "love, joy, peace, longsuffering, kindness, goodness, faithfulness, gentleness, self-control" (Galatians 5:22–23).

Ultimately, we need to surrender to God. That is the theme that runs through every season of your making. Submitting to God is insurance against sin. If we submit to God and resist the devil, the devil will flee (see James 4:7). The devil might not flee immediately, but he will flee. When you submit to God—when you submit to the principles of the Word and the Spirit—you are resisting the devil.

Youthful lusts and carnal lusts are resistible. When lust comes knocking on the door of your mind, do not ignore it. Confront it with the weapons of your warfare, which "are not carnal but mighty in God for pulling down strongholds"—including lust (2 Corinthians 10:4). If you pursue holiness, you will soon find freedom from sin, and God can increase the prophetic anointing on your life.

The Message's rendering of James 4:7–10 brings this home:

Let God work his will in you. Yell a loud *no* to the Devil and watch him scamper. Say a quiet *yes* to God and he'll be there in no time. Quit dabbling in sin. Purify your inner life. Quit playing the field. Hit bottom, and cry your eyes out. The fun and games are over. Get serious, really serious. Get down on your knees before the Master; it's the only way you'll get on your feet.

9

Purging Prophetic Pride

In my editorial role at *Charisma* magazine, I come across all kinds of people. There are many among the nameless, faceless generation who walk in a level of humility and honor that I aspire to. Then there are prophetic prima donnas, divas, the all-out "exalted prophetesses" who walk in pride and pretense and seem to care little who knows it.

How do Christians with international ministries, book deals and large staffs become such drama queens (and kings) who think more highly of themselves than they ought? Did they start their journeys as part of the nameless, faceless generation only to fall victim to pride's puffery? Or were they always secretly striving for the spotlight? Were they always ready to climb over (or trample on) anyone and everyone to get to the top of the prophetic ministry ladder? What causes some prophets to abuse the people around them once they have "arrived" at a position of authority?

Every time I run into one of these prophetic prima donnas I walk away with the fear of God inside me, because I know that anyone can be deceived by the pride of life. Especially when success keeps knocking louder and louder. Especially when no one is willing to hold us accountable for the pattern of pride that manifests consistently in our lives. And especially when we fail to cooperate purposefully with the grace of God to peel off layers of pride as the Holy Spirit opens our eyes to this sin.

We can fall into pride any number of ways. Only a proud prophet would suggest that he does not still walk in a measure of pride. Pride is like an onion: There are many layers. Pride is not solely a temptation for prophets, of course—the apostle Paul said that "knowledge puffs up" (1 Corinthians 8:1)—it is also a mentality that can keep you in the wilderness longer than you need to be. Always remember: God "resists the proud, but gives grace to the humble" (James 4:6).

Part of the making process is willfully purging your soul of prophetic pride. In order to accomplish God's best and highest plan for your life—and in order to avoid the pit of destruction that pride will lead you into—you need to strive to have the same mind Jesus had. Jesus had the mind of a humble servant who knew who He was and what He was called to do. There is true power in humility. If you walk in humility, God will use you in greater ways than you could ever imagine.

Identifying Spiritual Pride

The first and worst cause of error that prevails in our day is spiritual pride. So said Jonathan Edwards, a preacher, theologian and missionary to Native Americans who lived in the 1700s. Edwards went on to say that spiritual pride is the main door by which the devil comes into the hearts of those who are zealous for the advancement of Christ—the chief inlet for smoke from the bottomless pit to darken the mind and mislead one's judgment, and the main handle by which Satan takes hold of Christians to hinder a work of God.

Those are powerful words for people walking in prophetic ministry. If those words were true in Edwards' day—and they were—then how much more are they true in our day! Think about it for a minute. In Edwards' era, there were no glittering mega-churches, no Facebook pages where popular preachers could update millions of "fans," no global satellites to broadcast prosperity messages to the masses and no Hollywood Christianity with all its trappings. In Edwards' era, rather, Europeans were fleeing to North America, in part, to gain freedom from oppressive religious systems.

In the modern prophetic ministry, we see spiritual pride because of position, spiritual pride because of prominence, spiritual pride because of popularity . . . even if the position, prominence and popularity are acquired only in a small local church. To be sure, the spiritually proud prophet does not need a large kingdom to call his own in order to feel superior. Regardless of how much influence he actually holds, the spiritually proud prophet sees himself as more discerning, more anointed, more eloquent, more revelatory, more important and, otherwise, well, more spiritual than everybody else.

Make sure that is not you.

How can you discern if you are walking in pride? Some of the ways spiritual pride manifests include self-righteousness, hypercritical attitudes, hypocrisy, scorning correction or guidance, putting on pretenses and false humility. God hates pride in any form, of course, but I believe spiritual pride is the worst manifestation. Spiritual pride is so deceptive that the one who walks in it is too proud to consider that he may be suffering from this deplorable disease.

Let's be clear: Just because people fall down and vibrate on the floor after you lay hands on them does not mean that God is pleased with your heart attitude. The Spirit moves in response to the faith present in the hearts of hungry people who come looking for God. Even miracles, signs and wonders do not validate a spiritually proud prophet's stance. It may take years or even decades, but make no mistake: If the spiritually proud prophet does not repent God will eventually bring him low. Take the time now to ask the Holy Spirit to show the prideful attitudes He wants you to lay down—and then repent and ask for the grace to walk in humility.

God Will Not Share His Glory

As part of the making process, embrace every lesson in humility that you encounter and set your heart right now never to touch God's glory. Jesus called you into the prophetic, and the Holy Spirit equipped you with the anointing and the gifts to operate in His Kingdom. You did not do anything to earn it and you do not deserve any credit for it. God will not give His glory to another (see Isaiah 48:11). One of the fastest ways to find yourself back in the wilderness is to touch His glory.

Consider Nebuchadnezzar. By the grace of God this Babylonian king grew and became strong—his greatness reached to the heavens and his dominion to the ends of the earth (see Daniel 4:20). Yet Nebuchadnezzar let spiritual pride into his heart. Daniel warned him to "break off your sins by being righteous, and your iniquities by showing mercy to the poor" (Daniel 4:27). But the proud king ignored the humble prophet.

A year later, Nebuchadnezzar was walking about the royal palace of Babylon when he said, "Is not this great Babylon, that I have built for a royal dwelling by my mighty power and for the honor of my majesty?" (Daniel 4:30). No sooner had those words departed from his mouth than Nebuchadnezzar's kingdom departed from him. He wound up dwelling with the beasts of the field, eating grass. God had given Nebuchadnezzar space to repent for trying to take glory that was not his. Since he refused, God cut off the honor that fed Nebuchadnezzar's spiritual pride.

Then there is King Herod.

> Now Herod had been very angry with the people of Tyre and Sidon; but they came to him with one accord, and having made

Blastus the king's personal aide their friend, they asked for peace, because their country was supplied with food by the king's country. So on a set day Herod, arrayed in royal apparel, sat on his throne and gave an oration to them. And the people kept shouting, "The voice of a god and not of a man!"

Then immediately an angel of the Lord struck him, because he did not give glory to God. And he was eaten by worms and died.

Acts 12:20–24

King Herod had exhibited pride for decades, and God's grace eventually ran out.

Curing Spiritual Pride

By contrast, humble prophets of the Lord would not touch God's glory with the proverbial ten-foot pole. When Peter entered the home of Cornelius, a centurion who had invited him to come and share the Gospel, Cornelius fell down at his feet and began to worship him. "But Peter lifted him up saying, 'Stand up; I myself am also a man'" (Acts 10:26). Peter knew better than to touch God's glory. In humility, he preached the Gospel to the Gentiles—reasoning that God is no respecter of persons—and many were saved to the glory of God.

In Lystra, Paul and Barnabas faced a similar situation. When Paul observed that a man who was crippled from birth had faith to be healed, he told the man to stand up on his feet. The healing power of God met the man at the point of his faith and healed him. When the people of Lystra saw what happened, they called Paul *Hermes* and Barnabas *Zeus* and intended to sacrifice oxen to them.

But when the apostles Barnabas and Paul heard this, they tore their clothes and ran in among the multitude, crying out and saying, "Men, why are you doing these things? We also are men

75

with the same nature as you, and preach to you that you should turn from these useless things to the living God, who made the heaven, the earth, the sea, and all things that are in them."

Acts 14:14–15

Paul could have chosen to take the glory for himself; instead, he ended up getting stoned when Jews arrived from Antioch and Iconium and turned the people against him. They left him for dead, but God had another plan for a man who refused to take glory that was not his.

Edwards taught that spiritual pride is "the main spring or at least the main support of all other errors. Until this disease is cured, medicines are applied in vain to heal all other diseases." The good news is that spiritual pride can be cured. The prescription is a strong dose of conviction, repentance and humility—and I might say an ongoing effort to cooperate with the grace of God to walk in the fear of the Lord.

It is interesting to note that Edwards is credited with playing a key role in the First Great Awakening that swept Europe and the young colonies in America. While there is plenty of talk about another Great Awakening and the healing of our land, I believe any widespread move of God is going to start with you and with me. We need to work with the Holy Spirit to root out spiritual pride and walk in humility so that we are prepared when God answers our cries to show us His glory.

So embrace the grace of humility in your making process. It will pay dividends when God exalts you as a voice of influence. Build an accountability team around you—people you trust who can give you a gentle rebuke if they see you beginning to pursue the path of a prophetic prima donna. Have no part of being a Lone Ranger prophet who is too good to give ear to wise counsel. If you want to emerge from the wilderness with a strong prophetic voice, ask the Holy Spirit to cultivate meekness in your heart now.

10

Rejecting a Judgmental Spirit

When Hurricane Katrina slammed into New Orleans in 2005, the city was devastated. Nearly 1,500 people died. Four hundred thousand jobs and 275,000 homes were lost—as well as many churches. Looting was out of control. Indeed, Hurricane Katrina cost the United States about $110 billion.

Hurricane Katrina was a tragedy—yet in the face of the devastation, prophets were actually competing for bragging rights over who prophesied it first and with the greatest accuracy. This is not the Spirit of Christ; nor is it the spirit of a mature prophet who knows the love of Christ. Prophetic ministry is not a competition. True prophets, at the slightest prophetic impression of a deadly storm approaching, would move immediately into deep intercession; they would not be focused on spotlighting their credibility in the aftermath. Jesus prophesied judgments against the Temple (see Matthew 24:2), but when the Temple was destroyed in AD 70, He did not appear supernaturally to the disciples to boast about His prophetic prowess.

Along with the quickness of claiming credit, there were prophets who determined that this tragedy was God's judgment on a wicked city—or on the United States itself. Again we look to Jesus' example. Jesus told His disciples that the eighteen people who died when the tower of Siloam fell on them were no worse sinners than other men who lived in Jerusalem at the time (see Luke 13:1–5). In other words, God's judgment was not the reason for the tower collapsing and killing those people.

I am not saying God cannot or does not discipline nations and peoples to wake them up. I *am* saying that we should not be so quick to declare the judgment of God. And I am also saying that if God's judgment does come, the appropriate response is not to rush to your computer and start sending emails and publishing blog posts about how you predicted it first. A quick computer search turns up many such articles about terrorist attacks, hurricanes and various other natural disasters. That sort of behavior relegates prophets to the likes of Nostradamus—the French pharmacist who published collections of prophecies in the 1500s—or the five-dollar psychic on the boardwalk.

Immature prophets are quick to offer strong words of correction and rebuke. They forget that the guidelines for personal prophecy are edification, exhortation and comfort (see 1 Corinthians 14:3). Personal prophecy, in other words, is supposed to strengthen, encourage and comfort people. The Amplified Bible says prophecy "speaks to men for their upbuilding and constructive spiritual progress and encouragement and consolation." And *The Message* says that the prophet is "letting others in on the truth so that they can grow and be strong and experience [God's] presence."

True Prophets Have a Mercy Gift

Whether you are prophesying over one person or a nation, a judgmental spirit will pollute your utterances. Yes, God is a God of justice. But God is also slow to anger, filled with unfailing love and forgiving of every kind of sin and rebellion (see Numbers

14:18). The kindness of God leads people to repentance (see Romans 2:4). One reason some lost souls never come to the Father for forgiveness is because the devil has convinced them God will reject them. God does not reject anyone who comes to Him asking for forgiveness with a sincere heart.

Likewise, many Christians struggle with accepting the love and grace of God that empowers them to turn away from sin after they have missed the mark. God is not looking for opportunities to judge and condemn people. He is looking for opportunities to love and bless people.

An important aspect of prophetic ministry is to turn the hearts of people toward the Father (see Malachi 4:5–6). You cannot usher people into the Father's loving embrace if you minister through a judgmental, critical spirit. If you find it easy (or if you enjoy) giving corrective prophetic words or declaring judgment, then you do not have a deep enough revelation of God's grace and goodness. Prophets should not take pleasure in announcing bad news. If you receive a prophecy of judgment against a person, city or nation, you should stand in the gap as Moses and Abraham did. You should begin interceding rather than running to your keyboard to compose an article.

When God told Moses He was going to destroy Israel and birth a nation through him that was mightier and greater, Moses did not get puffed up and say, "Awesome! Go get 'em, God, and make me great! These people are driving me crazy anyway. Blast them!" No, Moses kept prostrating himself before the Lord for forty days and forty nights and prayed that God would not destroy Israel (see Deuteronomy 9:25–29). Likewise, Abraham interceded for Sodom and Gomorrah, which were especially wicked (see Genesis 18:16–32). That is the spirit of a prophet. A true prophet will stand in the gap between sinful man and God and plead for His mercy despite the wickedness.

If you receive a word of judgment, you should intercede and even weep over what grieves God's heart. If you are critical and judgmental, you will struggle, like Jonah, to show mercy. Furthermore, you will find that God cannot trust you to prophesy in His name. Judgmental prophets may go forth in His name, but that does not mean He sent them. God is the judge, but He is not judgmental. If you are judgmental, people in the local church will run the other way when you make an altar call. No one wants to be torn down. We get enough of that in the world. Remember, it is one thing to bring a word of correction and sound the alarm. It is something else altogether to do it with a critical, judgmental spirit.

Seeing Clearly

In the Sermon on the Mount, Jesus made it clear that we must love people rather than judge them. Yes, there are true rebukes of the Spirit and genuine calls to repentance. But, as I have stated, the prophet's response to God's impending discipline should be a cry for mercy. If you find satisfaction in the judgment, you are flowing in self-righteousness or spiritual pride.

Whether we judge, criticize and condemn through public prophecies or keep the matter in our own hearts, God hears it all. And every drop of scorn we pour on another is being collected in a bucket of belittlement that will one day tip over and drench us with detraction. In other words, as *The Message* says, that critical spirit has a way of boomeranging (see Matthew 7:2). James put it this way: "Judgment is without mercy to the one who has shown no mercy. Mercy triumphs over judgment" (James 2:13).

In the Sermon on the Mount, Jesus said:

> "Do not judge so that you will not be judged. For in the way you judge, you will be judged; and by your standard of measure, it will be measured to you. Why do you look at the speck that is in your brother's eye, but do not notice the log that is in your own eye? Or how can you say to your brother, 'Let me take the

speck out of your eye,' and behold, the log is in your own eye? You hypocrite, first take the log out of your own eye, and then you will see clearly to take the speck out of your brother's eye."

Matthew 7:1–5 NASB

Some years ago, I believe the Lord gave me a revelation of what that "log" is: It is a log of judgment. Jesus did not say we should not try to get the speck out of our brother's eye. He just wants us to go about it with the right spirit. He wants us to get that log of judgment out of our eyes so we can see clearly— through the eyes of love—to help our brother get the speck out of his eye. Much the same, prophecy should be rooted in love, not judgment.

Getting to the Root of the Issue

Just as John the Baptist laid an axe to the root of the tree, you need to lay an axe to the root of a judgmental spirit in your heart that pollutes your prophecies. When God delivers "the word of the Lord" to a prophet, it starts off pure. David wrote: "The words of the LORD are pure words, like silver tried in a furnace of earth, purified seven times" (Psalm 12:6). But if the prophet's heart is not pure, then the prophetic utterance becomes much like a game of Chinese Whispers.

Maybe you played Chinese Whispers as a child. Here is how it works. Everyone sits in a circle. One person whispers a message into the ear of the next person, who then whispers it into the ear of the next person, and so on and so on. The last person in the circle speaks out loud the message that he or she received, and, almost without exception, it varies from the original. Sometimes it is completely different from the original message. "The milk man delivered some milk," for example, may come out at the end of the circle sounding something like "That bad man was ridden with guilt."

81

Look at that circle of people as the layers in your soul—your soul is your mind, will and emotions—that filter the prophetic message before you speak it. When the Holy Spirit whispers a message to your heart, it will not come out of your mouth accurately if it has to pass through layers of wrong mindsets about God or about people.

As humans with a sin nature still living in the flesh, we are at a disadvantage to begin with. We know that the "heart is deceitful above all things, and desperately wicked" (Jeremiah 17:9). We also know that the tongue is "an unruly evil, full of deadly poison" (James 3:8). That is why prophets have to press in to build an intimate relationship with God that helps break down wrong mindsets about who He is and how He operates. If we look at God as a judgmental boss waiting to hit someone over the head with a hammer, that will be reflected in how we deliver prophecies.

Weeding Out Religion and Bitterness

I believe that judgmental prophecies have two roots: "religion" and bitterness. The spirit of religion is legalistic—and if you break its rules you will be judged. Religion is performance-oriented. If you fail to live up to its standards, it condemns you. Jesus noted that the scribes and Pharisees of His day—the epitome of the religious spirit—"neglected the weightier matters of the law: justice and mercy and faith" (Matthew 23:23).

Prophets flowing in a religious spirit appear righteous, but their hearts are full of hypocrisy and lawlessness. They like the attention they get when they preach, pray and prophesy. Now, note that failing to live up to the intentions of your heart does not make you a hypocrite. That is where grace comes in. You become a hypocrite when you are not trying wholeheartedly to live up to what you preach. Religious pride causes you not to notice the log in your own eye, but to notice every little itsy bitsy teeny tiny speck in everyone else's eyes—and to judge them harshly for it.

Along with a spirit of religion, a root of bitterness can also breed a judgmental prophet. *The Message* puts it this way: "You're not going to dip into a polluted mud hole and get a cup of clear, cool water, are you?" (James 3:12). If your heart is polluted with bitterness, your prophecies will also be polluted with bitterness. And that bitterness often manifests as judgment. Simon the sorcerer accepted Jesus as his Savior, and even got filled with the Holy Spirit, but the bitterness in his heart caused him to move in the wrong spirit. Simon tried to buy the power of the Holy Spirit. He failed to realize that he already had the power of the Holy Spirit. When Peter pointed out his actions, he said, "I see that you are poisoned by bitterness and bound by iniquity" (Acts 8:23).

Pursue peace and holiness with everyone, and be on guard that no root of bitterness has an opportunity to spring up in your heart because it can corrupt many—including those to whom you prophesy (see Hebrews 12:14–15).

The spirit of religion and root of bitterness will breed judgmental prophets—and can also lead into the realm of false prophecy. Paul told the Ephesians to exchange bitterness for kindness, tenderheartedness and forgiveness (see Ephesians 4:31–32). That is the heart of Christ—and that should be the heart with which the prophet ministers.

11

Renouncing Rebellion, Stubbornness, Control and Manipulation

The story of Jonah's experience in the belly of a whale may be a kids' church favorite, but there are serious warnings here for New Testament prophets. Deeper examination of this familiar narrative reveals two spiritual death knells for prophets: rebellion and stubbornness. They are close kin to control and manipulation.

Let's look at the story. The Lord told Jonah to go to Nineveh and preach against the wickedness of its society. Jonah's immediate response was to run away from the Lord and board a ship that was headed in the opposite direction—toward Tarshish. A judgmental Jonah rebelled against the word of the Lord because he wanted Nineveh to experience God's wrath instead of His mercy. Jonah knew that Jehovah would forgive the people there if his prophetic message spurred them to repentance.

Prophets who rebel are in danger of tapping in to a spirit of divination and perverting the message God wants to deliver (see 1 Samuel 15:23). *Divination* is foretelling the future by occult means. Isaiah 44 declares that the Lord makes fools of diviners.

Similarly, prophets who embrace stubbornness are tapping in to idolatry (see 1 Samuel 15:23). And prophets who flow in control and manipulation are welcoming the influence of Jezebel in their lives and ministries.

Mature prophets understand the subtle workings of rebellion, stubbornness, control and manipulation in their hearts—and renounce them. The key word is *subtle*. Most prophets would not rebel against God blatantly, such as setting up idols or taking advice from Jezebel. The enemy seduces prophets with subtle forms of these sins to water down prophetic ministry. During the making process, the Holy Spirit will bring the refiner's fire to your soul—and you may see the dross of rebellion, stubbornness, control and manipulation manifest. At that point, you have a choice to make: Repent or stunt your prophetic growth.

Renouncing Rebellion and Stubbornness

A rebellious prophet cannot walk in his highest calling. Jonah is a good example of how a prophet can abandon his ministry to follow self-will into the wilderness. Indeed, rebellion and stubbornness made a fool out of Jonah, who brought danger to himself and those around him.

The Bible tells us that the ship carrying Jonah to Tarshish in his rebellion was about to be broken into pieces. The sailors were terrified for their lives. Meanwhile, Jonah was down in the hold of the ship taking a nap. Who could take a nap in the middle of such a violent tempest? Is it possible that Jonah's rebellion opened a door for a spirit of witchcraft to attack him? Spiritual witchcraft taps in to demonic powers. Fatigue, weariness and slumber are some of its manifestations. When witchcraft attacks, its victims may feel tired, oppressed or depressed. What could have caused Jonah to remain fast asleep in the midst of such a life-threatening situation? That is exactly what the ship's captain wanted to know.

So the captain went to him and said, "How can you sleep? Get up and call on your god!" (see Jonah 1:6). Jonah knew full well that he was in rebellion, but he was too stubborn to call upon his God. So the sailors drew lots to find out who was to blame for their misfortune. Only when the lot fell on Jonah did he acknowledge his rebellion. The sailors then asked Jonah what they could do to end the storm. Jonah told them to cast him into the furious sea. Indeed, Jonah chose to face certain death rather than repent. How stubborn can a prophet be?

The stubbornness of following self-will instead of God's will is idolatry and puts prophets in a precarious position. A vital part of the prophetic ministry is to see, hear and say. Psalm 115 makes it clear that everyone who trusts in idols takes on the characteristics of idols: "They have mouths, but they cannot speak; they have eyes, but they cannot see; they have ears, but they cannot hear" (Psalm 115:5–6 NASB). What good is a prophet who cannot speak, see or hear? About as good as a prophet who is in the belly of a whale.

And that is just where Jonah ended up when the sailors threw him into the tumultuous sea. His hellish situation eventually led him to call upon his God. Jonah recognized his rebellion and stubbornness and finally repented, acknowledging that, "Those who pay regard to false, useless, and worthless idols forsake their own [Source of] mercy and loving-kindness" (Jonah 2:8 AMPLIFIED).

Jonah promised God that he would obey, and the Lord delivered him from the whale's belly onto dry land. As the story goes, Jonah wound up preaching in Nineveh, the people repented—and he got mad. Despite his experience in the whale's belly, Jonah did not seem to learn his lesson. The end of the story is left to our imagination, but the Bible makes no record of the Lord using Jonah again.

I want to mention here in comparison the story of Jesus with His disciples in a boat during a violent storm (see Mark 4:36–41). Jesus was always in the perfect will of God. And it was Jesus who told the disciples, "Let us cross over to the other side" (verse 35). These men were with the Son of God, following His specific command. Thus, even though Jesus was asleep in the back of the storm-tossed boat, they should have known they were safe and should not have wavered in their faith. By contrast, we know that Jonah stepped out of God's will when he got into that boat heading the opposite direction from Nineveh.

Before we move in any direction, we need to be confident that we know God's will so that when the storms come we can respond appropriately. We can be in the center of God's will and face a storm. When we do, we rebuke it. But just as Jonah knew he was being willful—he did not have to pray about it—so we also know in our hearts when we are in willful rebellion.

My Smoking Bush

During my own season of rebellion, I cracked under the pressure of submitting to the making process. Sometimes the Lord will allow people in authority to place demands on you that seem unfair, unreasonable or undoable. And those demands may very well be unfair, unreasonable or undoable. Learning how to submit to spiritual authority—even spiritual authority that is self-serving and harsh—may be part of your making process.

When I cracked under the pressure of the ministry demands, I pulled a Jonah—I ran in the other direction. I did not end up in the belly of a whale, but I did have an encounter with a smoking bush and ride in an elevator with a blind man, through whom God made His message abundantly clear.

God was trying to get my attention during a time when I was rebelling against His plan. I could not see it. I saw only the injustice. I am sure it was not the first thing He tried, but what finally got my attention was smoke coming from a bush outside my condo. I circled the bush and investigated, expecting to find a cigarette butt somewhere near. No matter how hard I looked,

I could not find the source of the smoke. I finally gave up and got on the elevator, and rode to my stop with a blind man who slowly made his way off the elevator with his red-tipped cane.

That is when the Holy Spirit spoke to my heart: *You're blind*, He said. In my quest to do things my way, I had deceived myself. But God in His mercy forgave me when I repented. I learned that He is in control, and you cannot manipulate His plans. We have to do things His way.

I also learned that by submitting myself to harsh treatment from leaders, when God directed me to do so, I was inviting the presence of God into my life in a stronger way. Ultimately, it liberated me. Although God is not pleased with leadership that puts heavy loads on His people for personal gain, God is pleased when we suffer for His sake. If you are suffering at the hand of a leader, pray and—if God is telling you to stay—obey the Holy Spirit. As with King David, this might be part of your preparation process. Sometimes God will put you under a Saul to get the Saul out of you.

I know that I am extremely sensitive to the way I work with those in ministry under me—maintaining a culture of honor in my ministry—because I learned firsthand the frustration of spiritual abuse by leaders. Please note that in telling this story I am not giving you a mandate to place yourself under or remain under harsh leadership. Follow the Holy Spirit and you cannot go wrong.

Shunning Control and Manipulation

The only controlling and manipulative prophets you see in the Bible are false prophets. Think about it for a minute. False prophets come dressed as something they are not (see Matthew 7:15). False prophets prophesy lies in the name of the Lord (see Jeremiah 14:14). False prophets prophesy peace when repentance is required (see Jeremiah 16:16–17). False prophets fill us with false hope (see Jeremiah 23:17). False prophets prophesy when the Lord has not spoken (Jeremiah 23:21–22).

False prophets want to woo people to themselves in order to control them. They utter manipulative prophecies to get people to follow them instead of Jehovah. Control and manipulation are tools the enemy uses to pervert prophetic ministry. To control someone is to exercise restraining or directing influence over, or to have power over him. Prophets need to exercise self-control through the power of the Holy Ghost, but have no business seeking to control anyone else. If you see traces of control and manipulation manifesting in your life, go on a crusade to rid yourself of these traits because they are earmarks of the Jezebel spirit.

Jesus told the church at Thyatira that He had a few things against them: "You allow that woman Jezebel, who calls herself a prophetess, to teach and seduce My servants to commit sexual immorality and eat things sacrificed to idols" (Revelation 2:20). Jezebel will pollute your prophecy and lead you into control, idolatry and immorality. For more on the Jezebel spirit, pick up my book *The Spiritual Warrior's Guide to Jezebel: How to Overcome the Spirit of Control, Immorality and Idolatry* (Chosen, 2013).

As we saw with Jonah, God in His mercy will work for a season with prophets who have deep character flaws. Although the way might not be easy, God does not give up quickly. He is patient to reveal His heart and teach His ways. Love always hopes. You might land in the proverbial belly of the whale if God is giving you a revelation of any rebellion, stubbornness, control or manipulation within you. If you feel the pain of loss of intimacy with the Father and a dull spirit, beware: That could be a sign that you are headed into bondage to Jezebel. It is in your best interests to repent quickly and recommit yourself to a life of obedience. Anything else is misery. Remember, the last we saw of Jonah he was sitting under a gourd wishing he were dead.

12

Avoiding the Envy Trap

It really bothered me. Every year our church had a prophetic conference. I was presented opportunities to lead workshops on prophetic topics, but I was the only one on the prophetic teaching team whose name tag did not sport the title of *prophet* or *prophetess*.

Even though my name tag identified me as *minister*, I felt as though I was considered below par in the credibility department when it came to teaching about prophetic ministry. Year after year, for nearly a decade, I said nothing—and experienced disappointment every time the administrator presented me with my *minister* name tag.

Likewise, I was disappointed each and every year when I was not given room on the platform New Year's Eve to share the word of the Lord to our church. Often, the senior pastor gave the congregation the prophetic words the Lord had given me—and he did not acknowledge who had delivered the word. One time he even built an entire conference theme around a prophetic word I had shared with him privately.

See, I wanted people to know who had delivered those prophecies. I wanted the title. I wanted the recognition. Obviously, that was the wrong spirit. Obviously, I was not secure enough in my calling to exercise my gift without a title. (Well, I did exercise the gift without the title, but I was never happy about it.) I cannot tell you how many times in those early years I cried out to God asking Him to do something about this "title" issue. Finally, after some years of this repetitive prayer, He answered me with a one-liner: *I'm not going to allow people to address you by a title until it's no longer important to you.*

I finally got it. I was pursuing spiritual gifts and prophetic titles when I should have been pursuing the fruit of the Spirit and a servant's heart. I repented and got my heart right, and I have not been concerned about titles ever since. I am not against titles, per se. But there is such a focus on titles today, especially in apostolic and prophetic ministries, that it has gotten downright silly. I have met, for instance, *Chief Prophets* and *Most Exalted Prophetesses*. It is a ridiculous show of pride. By the time people started calling me *prophetess*, I was over the title chase. I would urge you to get over that title chase now. It is a stumbling block in the making process.

Envy Can Pervert the Prophetic

My issue was envy. Emerging prophets—or even established prophets—can fall prey to envy as they watch others in ministry receiving the recognition or honor they think they deserve. But here is the problem: An envious prophet is not trusting God for his promotion, and is, in fact, delaying it.

What does it mean to be envious? Merriam-Webster defines *envy* as "a painful or resentful awareness of an advantage enjoyed by another joined with a desire to possess that same advantage." Left unchecked, envy can quickly lead to its second definition: "malice." Can you see the danger? The Bible has plenty to say about envy.

"Envy slays a simple [person]" (Job 5:2). "Envy is rottenness to the bones" (Proverbs 14:30). The chief priests handed Jesus over to the Romans because of the envy in their hearts (see Mark 15:10). Paul warned us not to walk in envy but to put on the Lord Jesus Christ (see Romans 13:13–14), and pointed out that envy is a sign of carnality (see 1 Corinthians 3:3). "Love does not envy" (1 Corinthians 13:4). Envy is a work of the flesh (see Galatians 5:19–21). We are told not to envy one another (see Galatians 5:26). Peter said that we should lay envy aside (1 Peter 2:1).

James issued a challenge:

> If you have bitter envy and self-seeking in your hearts, do not boast and lie against the truth. This wisdom does not descend from above, but is earthly, sensual, demonic. For where envy and self-seeking exist, confusion and every evil thing are there.
>
> James 3:14–15

Can you imagine releasing a prophetic word through the veil of confusion and every evil thing? Envy can pervert the prophetic. Envious prophets quench the Spirit and often disqualify themselves from flowing in the anointing that sets the captives free because they themselves are captives.

Breaking the Bondage of Envy

In the early years of my call to prophetic ministry, I had a "painful or resentful awareness of an advantage" enjoyed by the other prophets in the church and a "desire to possess that same advantage." I was envious. And it got me nowhere. God was gracious and merciful to me, of course. But He would not let me advance to the next level of prophetic ministry until I renounced that envy and the covetousness associated with it.

Maybe for you it is not a title. Maybe you envy itinerant prophetic ministers who travel around the world speaking God's words. That may or may not be God's plan for your ministry, but you will not find out until you let go of the envy. Maybe you are envious of people with media platforms—TV, books or Internet columns—where they can share prophetic insights. That may or may not be God's plan for your ministry, but you will not find out until you let go of the envy. Maybe you are just envious of how another prophet flows in his or her gifting. That attitude will not get you a stronger anointing.

Remember, no two prophets are exactly alike. God has a unique plan for your life and ministry, and you can trust that His will for you is good, acceptable and perfect (see Romans 12:2). God once said:

> For I know the thoughts that I think toward you, says the LORD, thoughts of peace and not of evil, to give you a future and a hope. Then you will call upon Me and go and pray to Me, and I will listen to you. And you will seek Me and find Me, when you search for Me with all your heart.
>
> Jeremiah 29:11–13

God spoke those words to Israel when she was facing captivity in Babylon. But the same could be said to prophets whom the enemy has taken captive. God wants to exalt you, but you first have to humble yourself.

I will never forget the day my mentor, who had been walking in prophetic ministry for decades, told me she considered me her equal. That was true humility on her part. Clearly, I did not have the experience or wisdom she possessed. But she was honoring me as one who had been through fire and become humbled enough to walk alongside her in this vital ministry. I had broken free of the bondage of envy.

Count Your Blessings

Envy grows from an ungrateful spirit. We should be thankful to God for the gifts and opportunities He has given us—not coveting someone else's title, status, platform or flow. God has blessed us with every spiritual blessing in heavenly places in Christ (see Ephesians 1:3). He saved us from eternal hell fire. He loves us so much that He gave us His Word to light our path, His Spirit to lead and guide us into truth and His authority to enforce His will on earth.

Envy warps your perspective of the truth and causes you to focus on what the enemy shows you instead of what God wants you to see. The late Associated Press humor columnist Harold Coffin once said, "Envy is the art of counting the other fellow's blessings instead of your own." There is a lot of truth in that. Rather than focusing on what the other prophet has that you want, why not focus on cultivating the unique prophetic gifting God gave you? After all, is the gift meant to glorify God or to glorify you? Prophecy should exalt Jesus, not any human.

Dietrich Bonhoeffer, German Lutheran pastor, theologian and anti-Nazi resistant, put it this way: "God's truth judges created things out of love, and Satan's truth judges them out of envy." How can a prophet flow in envy and expect to deliver God's pure word to peoples and nations? The prophetic wisdom envy brings is rooted in the earthly, sensual and demonic because, as James said, "Where envy and self-seeking exist, confusion and every evil thing are there" (3:16).

Instead of looking at what other prophets have, or how their callings manifest, why not look to Jesus, the Author and Finisher of your faith? Why not focus on God's Word? Why not spend your energy in prayer? Why not just go out and serve in any capacity you can? In other words, get your mind off yourself and what you "lack"—get your mind off others and what they have that you want—and get about the Father's business. The harvest is ripe and the laborers are few. Show yourself faithful with the talents God gave you, and He will bring increase to your ministry in due season.

Moving in the Opposite Spirit

I was transparent enough to share with you my hang-ups about titles and platforms that plagued me early in my prophetic ministry. What about you? Can you be that honest with yourself? Remember, lying to yourself will not get you where you want to go. Examine your heart for the green-eyed monster called envy and repent if you find it hiding there. Then, decide in your contrite heart to move in the opposite spirit so that God can promote you in the prophetic in His timing. When you move in the opposite spirit, you avoid the bondage of envy—for envy is bondage.

So what does it mean to move in the opposite spirit of envy? In a word, *blessing*. James made it clear that the wisdom that comes from bitter envy and self-seeking is earthly, sensual and demonic. But he also gave us a contrast:

> The wisdom that is from above is first pure, then peaceable, gentle, willing to yield, full of mercy and good fruits, without partiality and without hypocrisy. Now the fruit of righteousness is sown in peace by those who make peace.
>
> James 3:17–18

If you are envious of someone because he has a prophetic position, title, ministry or flow that you want, why not bless that person rather than resenting him in your heart? I overcame envy, in part, by blessing the prophets in my congregation who had the titles and platforms I wanted. I bought them Bibles, took them to dinner, helped them with small tasks and so on. In doing so, I was able to spend time with prophetic people who had already experienced the growing pains I was feeling—and I learned a great deal about how to walk in prophetic ministry.

13

Identifying (and Eliminating) Wrong Motives

I chose Jesus, but I never chose prophetic ministry. Jesus chose me—an unlikely candidate—to offer His mind and will via a multimedia platform. I still cannot figure out why. I prefer not to have attention focused on me. I was painfully shy as a child and still am far from the bubbliest personality in the bunch. I was never graduated from any seminary. I never even got a college degree. I am among the least likely, from a natural perspective, to speak into people's lives every day.

Yet God interrupted my well-laid plans and directed me to build a media ministry. I was prepared in "Egypt" (trained in the world to serve in the Kingdom), learning multimedia skills that would help me get His message out to millions of people a year.

Since God has put prophetic anointing on my writing, I could get into serious trouble if my motives strayed from the desires of His heart. In other words, if I do not keep my motives right, the enemy could come in and pervert the voice God has given me and use my God-given platform to publish warped information.

Regardless of how God's prophetic anointing works through you—whether through media, song, preaching, etc.—it is up to you to keep your heart pure amid the many opportunities to pursue wrong motives that come your way during the making process. The prophetic ministry is not a Broadway play; nor is it a cash cow. Wrong motives can leave you wandering around in the wilderness or draw you into the cave of deception. As we have noted, the gifts and callings of God are irrevocable, which is why you see fallen prophets still prophesying lies through Christian media. Pure motives are essential to a pure prophetic ministry.

Checking Your Motives

You have probably seen a few prophetic showmen in your day. Some exaggerate stories about prophetic encounters to make themselves appear more spiritual. Others make an altar call and literally knock people down in attempts to create what looks like powerful prophetic encounters. Still others put on a prophetic display in the prayer room.

The motive of these hypocrites is to be admired by men—and they have their reward through those who marvel at their dedication to prayer. Maybe they want to prove what fierce spiritual warriors they are by shouting the loudest at the prayer meeting.

There is nothing wrong with praying in public, obviously. It is the heart motivation that matters. Take care: Get your heart right before you preach, pray and prophesy. People might not see through the theatrics, but God does. I don't know about you, but I would rather receive God's slight nod over man's standing ovation. And you get more than God's slight nod when His Kingdom purposes motivate your heart.

John the Baptist never looked for personal gain through his ministry; he sought to exalt Christ (see John 3:30). And Christ did not use His spiritual gifts to raise offerings—in fact, He wove a whip and drove the merchandisers out of the house of prayer.

Prophets who are driven by fame and fortune are not walking in the Spirit and do not consistently bear the fruit of the Spirit: love, joy, peace, forbearance, kindness, goodness, faithfulness, gentleness and self-control (see Galatians 5:22–23). There is no counterfeit for love—and love must be our motive.

Jesus put it this way: "When you pray, you shall not be like the hypocrites. For they love to pray standing in the synagogues and on the corners of the streets, that they may be seen by men" (Matthew 6:5). *The Message* drives home this point: "And when you come before God, don't turn that into a theatrical production either. All these people making a regular show out of their prayers, hoping for stardom! Do you think God sits in a box seat?"

Whether you are in the very beginning of the making process or you are a veteran prophetic minister, step back in time for a moment to the beginning. What was your motive for entering prophetic ministry? Be painfully honest with yourself. Ask the Holy Spirit to show you if you entered with any wrong motives. Chances are, if you entered prophetic ministry with wrong ideas and motives, you are still carrying them with you today. And if you are still carrying them with you today, the enemy could set you up for a fall.

Remember, Jesus has to call you to this office—and even when He does you still cannot make yourself a prophet. God has to make you. If you try to force His hand, you are basically inviting the enemy to give you a false anointing.

Where Promotion Comes From

The idea that all promotion comes from God is scriptural. David explained it in one of his psalms: "Exaltation comes neither from the east nor from the west nor from the south. But God is the Judge: He puts down one, and exalts another" (Psalm 75:6–7). Need another witness? Peter wrote: "Humble yourselves under the mighty hand of God, that He may exalt you in due time" (1 Peter 5:6). Here is one more witness for good measure: "Humble yourselves in the sight of the Lord, and He will lift you up (James 4:10).

Can you see the running theme here? Prophets are not supposed to seek fame and promotion; prophets are supposed to seek humility. If God wants you speaking on a national platform, He will open the door. If God wants people to recognize your gift at all, for that matter, He will reveal it. It is not up to you to devise clever marketing gimmicks to get your name out there or to manipulate your pastor into giving you a turn in the pulpit. It *is* up to you to take on the example of John the Baptist and trust God.

When John's disciples came running with the message that people were flocking to Jesus for baptism, the prophet did not start scrambling for a new program because his ministry was taking a hit. John answered them this way:

> "A man can receive nothing unless it has been given to him from heaven. You yourselves bear me witness, that I said, 'I am not the Christ,' but, 'I have been sent before Him.' He who has the bride is the bridegroom; but the friend of the bridegroom, who stands and hears him, rejoices greatly because of the bridegroom's voice. Therefore this joy of mine is fulfilled. He must increase, but I must decrease."
>
> John 3:27–30

That is the right attitude—and Jesus recognized his humility. Jesus said, "Among those born of women there has not risen one greater than John the Baptist" (Matthew 11:11). What a statement! Similarly, the Bible recognizes the prophet Moses as the meekest, humblest man on earth in his day (see Numbers 12:3). Humility does not promote itself and love is not self-seeking. We all want opportunities, of course, to use our prophetic gifts and talents. But I assure you that those opportunities are all around you. Start in your home. Start with your friends. Serve them and exalt Jesus. If you seek fame and promotion, you could very well get it. But your character will not keep you where the anointing takes you.

A Root of All Prophetic Evil

The pursuit of fame and the love of money often go hand in hand. I have heard stories of corrupted prophets literally throwing thousands of dollars of offering money up into the air over their heads and letting it shower down on them or rolling around in it on their hotel beds. And I have witnessed the prayer lines for a supposedly anointed $1,000 prayer shawl that "will take your prayer life to the next level." It is sickening, but it happens.

We know that "the love of money is a root of all kinds of evil"—and the Bible says "some have strayed from the faith in their greediness, and pierced themselves through with many sorrows" (1 Timothy 6:9–10). *The Message* puts it this way: "If it's only money these leaders are after, they'll self-destruct in no time. Lust for money brings trouble and nothing but trouble. Going down that path, some lose their footing in the faith completely and live to regret it bitterly ever after."

Prophetic ministry is not a business. I believe that God wants His people to prosper, but not through merchandising schemes that promise desperate believers breakthroughs in exchange for money—and not through websites that offer prophetic words for a "love offering" of at least fifteen dollars. I do not believe in selling prophetic words. A laborer is worthy of his wages, but the Bible clearly warns us to keep our lives free from the love of money and be content with what we have (see Hebrews 13:5).

Prophets, you cannot serve two masters. You cannot serve God and money (see Matthew 6:24). At some point along your prophetic path, you will likely be forced to make that choice.

If you choose money, it will compromise your message and you could become an earthen vessel of dishonor. You could even fall into the position of a false prophet. We know that the borrower is a slave to the lender (see Proverbs 22:7), and so the prophet who serves money becomes a slave to the source of that money. Like a drug addict, he will do anything to get it—even if it means selling out God's people to his lust. Ultimately, if you love money it will never satisfy you (see Ecclesiastes 5:10). You cannot obtain God's gifts with money, and you should not try to sell them, either.

"I'm Not Trying to Impress You"

People do all sorts of things to look more spiritual, more humble, more "whatever" than the other guy. The point is this: When you do something to impress people, you have your reward right then. Even if you start off in obedience to God and do something generous, like close the door on a ministry you have enjoyed, if you make a big deal about it—if you make sure everyone knows what you did so you can look like a sacrificial giver—you have received your reward in full.

You should ultimately be motivated by love for God and take an eternal view. When you look at your actions through an eternal lens, it becomes clearer what really matters and what really does not. If you behave as if an eternal God is watching—and He is—you develop fear of the Lord that leads to wisdom.

The rewards of man feel good at the moment, but even man's greatest rewards are fleeting. Ultimately, only God's rewards can satisfy our hearts. Anything that is not motivated by love will not last in eternity. Remember Paul's advice to the Corinthians, a church known for flowing in spiritual gifts:

> Love never fails. But whether there are prophecies, they will fail; whether there are tongues, they will cease; whether there

is knowledge, it will vanish away. For we know in part and we prophesy in part. But when that which is perfect has come, then that which is in part will be done away.

1 Corinthians 13:8–10

Love never fails. Let love be the motivation of your heart.

14

Overcoming Fear of Man

I once trembled at the thought of standing in front of a crowd, much less preaching, praying or prophesying in the spotlight. My hands shook. My mind wandered. My voice quavered. My legs wobbled. My stomach knotted. And my heart felt as if it was going to pound right out of my chest.

At the same time, I used to have such thin skin—I was so sensitive to criticism—that my heart ached when people would not receive my message. I have had to learn to toughen up over the years—especially to endure the verbal attacks from those who resist the words God has given me to say or write that hit a nerve. I have had to learn to overcome the fear of man in its many manifestations.

My perspective changed completely after the Holy Spirit broke into my emotional turmoil. He said, *Stop worrying about what other people think.* Sounds like a rather obvious revelation, but it shifted my mindset. This was not merely advice from a friend: The Spirit of God Himself was giving me a prophetic instruction to *Stop worrying about what other people think*, and the grace to obey came with that instruction.

See, when you worry about what other people think, you are giving them a measure of control over your life that belongs to the Holy Spirit. If you worry about what other people think, you set yourself up to become a people-pleaser rather than a God-pleaser. If you worry about what other people think, you might even give away some of your God-given identity. Indeed, you cannot function fully in your prophetic gift if you carry the weight of the fear of man on your back.

Let me put it another way: Fear of man can hinder you from prophesying the will of the Lord. If you are concerned about what people think, how can you deliver a word boldly? If you are not willing to deliver the unadulterated word of the Lord despite the persecution it could bring, then how can you prophesy over nations and peoples and governments? The Bible says we prophesy according to our faith (see Romans 12:6). The spirit of fear will battle your faith to silence your voice.

Fear Not, Prophet!

If you look at the calls and commissions of the Old Testament prophets, you see that God said one thing to many of them right up front: *Fear not*. He told Jeremiah not to be afraid "of their faces" (Jeremiah 1:8). He told Ezekiel not to be afraid "of their words or . . . their looks" (see Ezekiel 2:6). He told Daniel quite simply to "fear not!" (see Daniel 10:19).

Why did God tell His prophets not to fear? Because fear is one of the first weapons the enemy uses against prophets. He told Ezekiel not to look at their faces. Why? Well, have you ever stood up in front of a congregation and actually looked at the people's faces? Many of them look mad. Some of them look as though they are going to fall asleep. Others look completely blank. It can be scary up there if you have never overcome the fear of man.

Fear is a "ruling" spirit—it is one of the key spirits that have come against God's people since the beginning. This is why God exhorts us hundreds of times in Scripture not to fear. Fear is at the root of many other issues, like anxiety, worry and stress. You cannot fear man and fear the Lord at the same time. Fear is a spirit that speaks to our emotions to cause us to shrink back from what God has called us to do.

Fear is a weapon the enemy uses against prophets and prophetic people to keep their jaws tightly clamped. The devil uses it to get you to run to your cave instead of speaking what the Spirit of God says. It is also the tactic the devil uses to keep you from sharing vital prophetic insights. Fear, as a spirit, causes an emotional reaction. You cannot reach the heights of your prophetic gifting if the fear of man plagues your emotions.

The Bible says that "fear involves torment" (1 John 4:18). Fear is indeed a form of torment. And if the emotion of fear is not anguish enough, the devil follows it up with a heavy dose of condemnation. The same devil that tempted you with fear condemns you for being too timid to step out in faith and speak prophetically. "Without faith it's impossible to please God!" he whispers. "You just blew it again. God's going to find someone else to use!"

Have you ever been in an intercessory prayer gathering and felt the unction of the Holy Spirit to prophesy? You knew the Lord was speaking to you, but when the prayer leader called those with prophetic words to step forward, fear paralyzed you. Just a minute before, you were praying boldly with the rest of the intercessors at the prayer meeting, binding principalities and powers and wreaking havoc on the enemy's camp. Then suddenly "the word of the Lord came unto you saying . . ." and you ran into the bathroom to hide. Or you stood there struggling within yourself, trying to convince yourself to speak up before it was too late. That is a manifestation of the fear of man.

Fear of Man Invites Temptation

The wisest man in the world once said this: "The fear of man brings a snare, but whoever trusts in the LORD shall be safe" (Proverbs 29:25). *The Message* states: "The fear of human opinion disables; trusting in GOD protects you from that."

What kind of snare is God protecting you from when you refuse to bow to the fear of man? Replacing the word *snare* with *temptation* offers insight. The fear of man may tempt us not to trust God. It might lead to dishonesty. Abraham displayed the fear of man when he said that Sarah was his sister: Even though she was his half sister, he was implying that she was not his wife. The fear of man could tempt us to prophesy what people want to hear instead of what God is saying, as did many of the false prophets in Jeremiah's day. And, again, the fear of man could tempt us to remain silent when we know God wants us to speak.

These are snares, temptations that take you out of God's will. But there is greater danger: Fear of man can also lead you straight to witchcraft's door. When you fear man, you are subject to being manipulated and controlled by people who flow in a Jezebel spirit, which seduces you into immorality and idolatry. As a mouthpiece for God, you must be subject to the Holy Spirit, not Jezebel and her witchcraft. King Saul is a good example of how someone with a true ministry and anointing from God can fall into counterfeit spiritual authority, or witchcraft, by succumbing to this temptation.

Here is the scene: The Philistines, with an army of thirty thousand, were preparing to attack Israel. The men of Israel recognized the danger and hid. Saul was in Gilgal waiting for the prophet Samuel to come and make a sacrifice on the nation's behalf. When Samuel was late and the people began to scatter,

Saul took matters into his own hands and offered a burnt offering to the Lord. As soon as he did, Samuel arrived.

> And Samuel said, "What have you done?"
>
> Saul said, "When I saw that the people were scattered from me, and that you did not come within the days appointed, and that the Philistines gathered together at Michmash, then I said, 'The Philistines will now come down on me at Gilgal, and I have not made supplication to the LORD.' Therefore I felt compelled, and offered a burnt offering."
>
> 1 Samuel 13:11–12

In the King James Version, Saul says he "forced" himself. But it was fear of man that caused Saul to disobey. This disobedient act opened the door to an even greater sin later in Saul's rule. The Philistines were once again gathered against Israel. And once again, Saul "was afraid, and his heart trembled greatly. And when Saul inquired of the LORD, the LORD did not answer him, either by dreams or by Urim or by the prophets" (1 Samuel 28:5–6).

Since Samuel had died, Saul ordered his servants to find a medium he could consult. That medium was known as the witch of Endor. The lesson: If we receive our authority, recognition or security from man instead of God we could end up like Saul—in the witch's house.

Jesus offered instruction to prophetic people:

> "Whatever I tell you in the dark, speak in the light; and what you hear in the ear, preach on the housetops. And do not fear those who kill the body but cannot kill the soul. But rather fear Him who is able to destroy both soul and body in hell."
>
> Matthew 10:27–28

Fear of man and fear of God cannot coexist. While the fear of man brings a snare, the reverential fear of the Lord is the beginning of wisdom (see Psalm 111:10) and knowledge (see

107

Proverbs 1:7). Wisdom and knowledge are part and parcel of true prophetic ministries.

Jesus Was Not Afraid of Anyone

When Jesus healed the paralytic and forgave his sins, some of the scribes were sitting there thinking, "Why does this Man speak blasphemies like this? Who can forgive sins but God alone?" (Mark 2:7). Jesus knew what they were thinking, but that did not stop Him from healing the next guy. What if Jesus had worried about how it would look to heal and forgive on the Sabbath? What if Jesus had started picking and choosing when and whom and how He would heal based on the day of the week or how sinful the sinner was or who was watching? God forbid.

Jesus had a habit of casting out devils. After He healed a demon-possessed, blind and mute man, the Pharisees said, "This fellow does not cast out demons except by Beelzebub, the ruler of the demons" (Matthew 12:24). Did Jesus bring His deliverance ministry to a screeching halt because people with religious spirits accused him of casting out devils by the power of darkness? No, because He was not concerned about what His critics thought.

Do you imagine that Jesus was sitting up all night worrying about what people thought of His Sermon on the Mount? Hardly. Did everyone who heard it like it? Doubtful. Some "religious" people there surely launched all manner of accusations against the Word of God made flesh. That did not stop Jesus from speaking and doing the will of God. It is not going to stop me. And it should not stop you, either.

Overcoming the Fear of Man

If you recognize the fear of man in your soul, do not condemn yourself. Just commit to waging war against it. I prayed for a couple of years for a spirit of boldness. One day, I suddenly noticed a spirit of boldness in my ministry. If fear of man is tempting you, the first line of defense is prayer. Ask the Lord to give you "the Spirit of . . . the fear of the LORD" (see Isaiah 11:2). Ask Him to give you a spirit of boldness, and to deliver you from the spirit of fear.

Also, take action. Do not wait until you are free from fear to step out in faith to obey God. Action overwhelms fear, even if you have to do it when you are afraid. I share my prophetic insights and opinions in print every week. When I first started, I used to fear backlash. If I had not overcome that fear I would have stopped writing, because I certainly get some pretty nasty backlash at times. Any time you step out into something new you will probably feel the fear of man. But step out anyway. The battle is in the mind. Do not meditate on the fear. Do not entertain fearful thoughts.

Concentrate on God's will. Think about your love for God's people and His desire to speak to them. Be willing to sacrifice your own comfort to comfort His people. If your mind is on yourself and your fear, you will find it hard to deliver a word boldly. Sometimes it is the waiting that kills you. You have a word and are waiting for the platform to open—and the anxiety builds. Keep reciting the word of the Lord over and over until you have the opportunity to speak. Once you open your mouth and get going, the fear will usually leave you. It is that period of time right before you open your mouth that is the problem.

Tell yourself that the world will not come to an end if no one receives the word of the Lord you have delivered. Nobody is perfect: You might miss it. Or maybe the listeners cannot recognize the voice of the Lord when they hear it. Either way, you will survive. Remember, fear is not from God. Fear is from Satan: "God has not given us a spirit of fear, but of power and of love and of a sound mind" (2 Timothy 1:7). Every time you feel fear in your life, it is a manifestation of the kingdom of darkness. We can even begin to fear the spirit of fear if we fail to stand against this demonic attack.

You must not let fear rule your life. You must not let this spirit rob you of your prophetic destiny. Meditate on the love of God—God loves you. Perfect love casts out fear. Faith overcomes fear. We prophesy according to our faith. Be a prophet of faith. If you believe that the Lord truly spoke to you, then you can overcome prophetic stage fright and the fear of man. When you are faithful to walk in your true prophetic authority at this level—without compromising—then the Lord can trust you and promote you to the next level.

15

Responding to Rejection and Ridicule

If you have walked in the prophetic anointing any length of time, you have undoubtedly felt the pain of rejection. Dealing with that pain God's way is part of the making process. Old Testament prophets—and even Jesus Himself—had to deal with the reality that many would not receive their prophetic words. They were ridiculed and attacked for serving as God's oracles, speaking the revelations that God was giving.

As you keep your prophetic flow pure, you will face a measure of rejection. You will be overlooked, ridiculed or attacked for the God-inspired words that come out of your mouth or off your pen, while false prophets are celebrated. How you respond could make an eternal difference in your prophetic ministry.

The Bible offers clear examples of how various prophets responded when their messages were rejected. Let's look at two—Ahithophel and Agabus—who acted in stark contrast to one another: Ahithophel embraced a spirit of rejection to the point of death; Agabus let it go.

Ahithophel's Surprising Developments

Ahithophel was one of David's trusted advisors. Whether or not he was a prophet—some say yes, some say no—the Bible says that "every word Ahithophel spoke seemed as wise as though it had come directly from the mouth of God" (2 Samuel 16:23 NLT). Sure sounds as though he was a prophet to me.

In any case, David always followed Ahithophel's advice. Not sometimes. Not occasionally. Always. Can we agree that the discerning monarch would not have listened to Ahithophel if he had not consistently offered sage advice? Ahithophel had a good track record. He was an accurate mouthpiece for God.

Then something unexpected happened. When King David's eldest son, Absalom, organized a rebellion to take over the kingdom, David fled Jerusalem, and this trusted advisor betrayed him by staying behind and siding with the young gun. Ahithophel's defection was especially damaging to David because the counselor was so well regarded. When David discovered that Ahithophel had taken his loyalties to the enemy's camp, he asked the Lord to thwart his plans. He also sent the prophet Hushai to appear to give allegiance to young Absalom, but to actually work to counter Ahithophel's advice.

Ahithophel never saw it coming. He suggested a brilliant strategy for Absalom that would have meant certain defeat for King David, but the rebellious youth decided to summon Hushai to see what he had to say. Hushai wasted no time in telling Absalom, in effect, that Ahithophel was steering him in the wrong direction. Hushai offered much different advice—advice that appealed to Absalom's pride. Absalom took the bait. And so it was that the Lord answered David's prayer and discredited Ahithophel's wise counsel.

Ahithophel should have taken the time to seek God's face to ask if he had missed the mark, and if so, how and why. That is what every prophet should do when a prophetic word is rejected. Since prophets are human, a little bit of the human soul and spirit can get mixed in with the prophetic word. Or the prophet could be tapping in to idolatry in a recipient's heart. Or the prophet could be tapping in to some spirit besides the Holy One. Or, of course, the prophet could be accurate and the hearer could be missing it.

Ahithophel did not seek God, though. The Bible says that when Absalom rejected his prophetic counsel, Ahithophel saddled a donkey, took off to his hometown, put his household in order, hanged himself and died (see 2 Samuel 17:23). Ahithophel took Absalom's rejection of his counsel personally. That is never the correct response of a mature prophet. God is watching to see who is perfected to the point of utter humility. Ahithophel's response demonstrated character flaws that sidelined him and cost him his life.

Agabus' Better Example

In contrast to Ahithophel is the New Testament's Agabus. Through the means of prophetic demonstration, Agabus used the belt of the apostle Paul to tie his own hands and feet, and then declared that Paul would be similarly bound in Jerusalem and handed over to the Gentiles (see Acts 21:10–11). Agabus had a credible track record. This is the same prophet who had earlier predicted the famine (see Acts 11:27–28). Those who heard what the Holy Spirit said through Agabus received the word as true and pleaded with Paul not to go up to Jerusalem.

When they saw that Paul would not be dissuaded, however, they gave up and said, "The Lord's will be done." Agabus had fulfilled his prophetic duty by warning Paul. His job completed, Agabus joined the others and said simply, "The Lord's will be done." That was the proper response in the face of Paul's decision not to avoid capture. Unlike Ahithophel, Agabus did not take Paul's response as personal rejection. He simply moved on to his next assignment.

113

How Do You Handle Rejection?

How do you respond when someone does not receive a prophecy you deliver? Do you get offended and accuse the hearer of having dull spiritual ears? Do you get angry at the hearer's blight upon your prophetic reputation? Do you, like Ahithophel, feel rejected and run back to your cave, destined to break bread and sip water with the other prophets who cannot bear the shame of being wrong? Or do you take it to the Lord and ask Him for His perspective?

Listen, maybe you were right and maybe you were wrong. If you were right, then the Lord will vindicate you. Perhaps the person to whom you gave the prophecy will come to you and confirm the accuracy of the word. If you were wrong, and you keep a humble heart, perhaps the Lord will come to you and share His revelation of how you missed it so you do not make the same mistake again. Whether or not the hearer accepts the prophetic word of the Lord from your mouth, your response should be single-minded: "Let the Lord's will be done."

You Are Accepted in the Beloved

Sometimes you might feel rejection as a prophet, whether your words are received or not. Sometimes the rejection stems from life encounters that left you wounded. Rejection used to have a tight rein on my soul—and I did not even know it. All I knew was that I always felt as if something was wrong with me. I often assumed that nobody really cared. And I sometimes was sure that people were talking about me behind my back.

> Rejection works subtly to destroy your self-esteem and your purpose.
>
> Rejection causes you to feel sorry for yourself.

Rejection spurs you to reject other people before they have
an opportunity to reject you.

Rejection leads you to base your worth on what you do instead
of who you are in Christ.

There will be times, of course, that you deal with true rejection,
but there is also imagined rejection. Indeed, rejection often works
through imaginations: Hurtful encounters, for instance, can open
the door for a demon of rejection to whisper to you and torment
you. That spirit can twist your perception of circumstances so
that it looks and feels as though you are being rejected even when
you are not. In the natural, it is called a misunderstanding. But
if you fail to cast down the imaginations that ride on the back
of misunderstandings, the spirit of rejection will work to form
a stronghold in your mind. It will control your thought patterns
and make it easy for this demon to hold you in bondage.

Whether you are in full-blown bondage to rejection or just
have an occasional battle with this spirit, the remedy is the same:
Reject rejection and accept your God-given identity.

I remember a time when I was really beating myself up over
something. I was down on my knees virtually whipping myself
with self-condemning prayers. I was crying out to God over and
over about the same weakness, asking Him to forgive me and
wondering what was wrong with me. There was nothing really
wrong with me. I was just growing in character. But rejection
was doing a number on me.

Suddenly, in the midst of my self-rejection, I heard a still,
small voice that said, *Would you just stop it?*

That startled me. After all, I was on my knees praying from
my heart to the Father. Why would He want me to stop?

When I stopped, the Holy Spirit said, *How would you like to
watch your daughter sit there and beat herself up every morning?*

See, I was not praying. Not really. I was not approaching
the throne of grace boldly to receive mercy and find grace in

a time of need (see Hebrews 4:16). I was merely repeating to God the words that rejection had recited to me as if they were gospel truth. I was condemning myself for an innocent matter of immaturity.

As I sat there silently, tears still rolling down my cheeks, the Holy Spirit said, *Go read Ephesians 1:6.*

I have to admit that I did not know what that Scripture was going to say. I knew generally speaking that it had something to do with our redemption in Christ. I got off my sore knees and opened up my Bible. Ephesians 1:6 says: "He made us accepted in the Beloved."

Wow! That changed my whole perspective. God Himself interrupted my self-condemning thoughts to let me know that He accepts me with all my faults and all my immaturities. From that point on, I made it my mission to reject rejection and accept my God-given identity.

Silencing the Voice of Rejection

Whenever I hear rejection begin to whisper that no one cares—and the spirit of rejection will often take the opportunity to say things like that when you are walking through a fiery trial—I tell that devil something like this: "I cast all my cares upon the Lord, for He cares for me" (see 1 Peter 5:7). And my punch line is always: "I am accepted in the Beloved."

Chances are, you will have to reject rejection over and over in your prophetic ministry. Whether real or perceived, rejection does not just give up. If it cannot turn you into a self-pity-toting performer, rejection will puff you up with pride to compensate for your insecurities—or lead you to shield yourself with pat answers and not get involved to guard yourself from more rejection.

When rejection comes whispering to your soul, telling you that something is wrong with you—you are not "this" enough, "that" enough or "something else" enough—reject that thought in the name of Jesus. The truth is, you are fearfully and wonderfully made. You "are complete in Him, who is the head of all principality and power" (Colossians 2:10). You are God's "workmanship, created in Christ Jesus for good works" (Ephesians 2:10). So reject rejection and accept your God-given identity.

Be conscious of your thoughts. Any thought with even the slightest hint of rejection should be immediately cast down and replaced with the truth.

> The truth is God loves you (see Romans 1:7).
>
> The truth is you were delivered from the power of darkness and conveyed into God's Kingdom (see Colossians 1:13).
>
> The truth is you are forgiven of all your sins and washed in the blood (see Ephesians 1:7).
>
> The truth is you are the righteousness of God in Jesus Christ (see 2 Corinthians 5:21).
>
> The truth is when you are submitted to God, rejection has to flee from you when you resist it (see James 4:7).

I could go on and on and on. If you want to keep it really simple, do what I do. When a spirit of rejection comes whispering, I tell that devil: "I am accepted in the Beloved." And nothing else matters. Not really.

Reject rejection and accept your God-given prophetic identity in the name of Jesus!

16

Embracing the Glory of Persecution

I stayed in an abusive church for years because I feared the persecution that would chase me out the door if I dared to leave. I did not recognize the subtle signs of spiritual abuse while I was enduring the mistreatment, of course. I just knew that the pain of staying was growing worse than the fear of leaving.

When God opened my eyes to the spirits operating in that toxic church, I knew I could no longer endorse its teaching, support it financially or condone its cultish leadership paradigm. I had three choices: I could confront the leadership; I could warn the sheep; or I could walk away quietly, endure the persecution that would surely follow and refuse to look back.

After submitting my case confidentially to mature spiritual leaders outside that local church and praying fervently for weeks, I was led by the Holy Spirit into a process of forgiveness and then told to *Go in peace*. That meant no confrontation and no warning the sheep. That was difficult for me because one aspect of my prophetic calling is to confront sin by sounding the alarm.

My intention was to be obedient and go in peace, but when I informed the leadership of my decision to move on, there was nothing peaceful about their reaction. For my part, I went in peace—never exposing to the congregation what I knew as I prayed that God would deliver them out of bondage—but persecution by those in leadership chased me for years after I left.

Indeed, their response was so harsh that outsiders who witnessed the public attacks against me—including Facebook posts and YouTube videos—described it as "emotional terrorism" and "psychological warfare." When members of the congregation asked leaders why I had left, they were led to believe that I had fallen into sin and needed prayer. Concerned congregants were told never to contact me again. Obviously, some reached out anyway, but I still kept my peace.

And on it went. After I left, those leaders launched a preaching series about deception. Because I had been highly visible in the church's prophetic ministry and was suddenly gone, the congregation knew I was the subject of the sermons. Granted, the leaders did not mention my name, but no one had any question that they were talking about me. In tear-filled sermons the leaders suggested that a "false prophet" who had recently left the church—a Jezebel—had turned her back on Jesus. They warned the people not to let this or any other false prophet lure them out of the church.

These abusive pastors did not know that people were telling me about the public and private character assassination. I wish I had not heard these things, and had to ask people to stop telling me. Let's just say I had to learn to walk out the Beatitudes at a whole new level. I had to learn to embrace the glory of persecution. Some who witnessed my response to the persecution, or rather my lack of response, soon worked up the strength to leave the abusive system themselves.

Blessed Are the Reviled

What does *persecution* mean? Merriam-Webster defines *persecute* as "to harass or punish in a manner designed to injure, grieve or afflict; to cause to suffer because of belief." That certainly describes what I went through—and it may describe what you are facing or have already faced (and will likely face again).

Although it is not usually identified as spiritual abuse, the enemy uses people to launch persecution against true prophets. The enemy wants you to abort the call on your life altogether—or at least compromise it in some way. Both Jesus and Paul prophesied about the persecution believers would face. Jesus said: "If they persecuted Me, they will also persecute you" (John 15:20). And Paul said: "All those who desire to live a godly life in Christ Jesus will be persecuted." James brought it home to the prophetic when he wrote: "My brethren, take the prophets, who spoke in the name of the Lord, as an example of suffering and patience" (James 5:10).

In my editorial role at *Charisma*, I speak out on issues coming against the Gospel of Christ. Although most readers offer a hearty "Amen," I get reviled on a near-daily basis. In response to my article about free abortions at a women's health center, for example, a reader called me a "religious monger, ill-educated, selfish, appalling, downright pathetic, hateful, judgmental, destroying human compassion, acceptance and coexistence"—and then blamed me for "not allowing the United States to move forward with science, reason and progress." Yes, it was a mouthful. It was persecution.

Persecution never feels good. But persecution is truly glorious if you understand the fruit it produces in your life when you embrace it and respond the way Jesus taught us in the Beatitudes. When you understand the role of persecution in the making of a prophet, you can decide not to waste the experience. When you are persecuted, you really are blessed. You have to choose to see it that way.

Jesus said:

"Blessed are those who are persecuted for righteousness' sake, for theirs is the kingdom of heaven. Blessed are you when they revile and persecute you, and say all kinds of evil against you falsely for My sake. Rejoice and be exceedingly glad, for great is your reward in heaven, for so they persecuted the prophets who were before you."

Matthew 5:10–12

I like the way *The Message* expresses these verses:

"You're blessed when your commitment to God provokes persecution. The persecution drives you even deeper into God's kingdom. Not only that—count yourselves blessed every time people put you down or throw you out or speak lies about you to discredit me. What it means is that the truth is too close for comfort and they are uncomfortable. You can be glad when that happens—give a cheer, even!—for though they don't like it, *I* do! And all heaven applauds. And know that you are in good company. My prophets and witnesses have always gotten into this kind of trouble."

When Your Pastor Persecutes You

Pastors do not always understand or embrace prophets. A wise man once told me: "God will sometimes put you under a Saul to get the Saul out of you." Saul was Israel's first king, but when he disobeyed the Lord's command, God sent the prophet Samuel to anoint a new king. That new king was a young shepherd boy named David.

Samuel anointed David seventeen years before he actually took the throne—and David faced serious persecution before and after he was crowned. A jealous Saul wanted David dead. David was a fugitive for years. While on the run, David penned psalms that give us insight into his emotions: "O LORD my God, in You I put my trust; save me from all those who persecute me; and deliver me, lest they tear me like a lion, rending me in pieces, while there is none to deliver" (Psalm 7:1–2).

Despite years of persecution at Saul's hand, David chose to return good for evil. David had two opportunities to kill Saul. His men prophesied the murder as the will of the Lord both times, but David was a man after God's own heart and refused to move outside of His command.

The first time David stumbled upon Saul he was sleeping. Rather than murdering him and taking the kingdom by force, David secretly cut off a corner of Saul's robe—and even that troubled his heart. "He said to his men, 'The LORD forbid that I should do this thing to my master, the LORD's anointed, to stretch out my hand against him, seeing he is the anointed of the LORD'" (1 Samuel 24:6).

David's second opportunity came when Saul was asleep in the camp, his spear stuck in the ground next to his head. David would not take matters into his own hands. He told his soldiers:

> "Do not destroy him; for who can stretch out his hand against the LORD's anointed, and be guiltless?" David said furthermore, "As the LORD lives, the LORD shall strike him, or his day shall come to die, or he shall go out to battle and perish. The LORD forbid that I should stretch out my hand against the LORD's anointed. But please, take now the spear and the jug of water that are by his head, and let us go."
>
> 1 Samuel 26:9–11

From a natural perspective, David was in serious danger. Saul's army roamed about like a roaring lion seeking to devour him. But God's hand was on David's life. God allowed the persecution to shape David's character and mold him into a king who would fully trust and obey His commands—the opposite of Saul. God ultimately did not allow Saul to harm David. Remember this when you are in the throes of spiritual warfare, persecution and various other trials.

When you find yourself persecuted by spiritual leaders, it is time to press in to God as never before. You need to discover what the will of the Lord is. Should you stay and endure the persecution? Should you leave and let everybody know why on the way out the door? Should you exit in silence and wait for God's vindication?

There is no blanket answer. I believe there are times when God will have you stay in an unpleasant situation so you can learn something. If He calls you to leave, He may indeed have you warn others on the way out. In my case, I left quietly. Although my reputation among them was murdered, God soon enough exposed the truth.

When you are facing persecution, remember that you are not alone. Jesus said that the prophets who came before you have faced the same treatment. In order to put the persecution into perspective, go read about the suffering of Jeremiah, Isaiah or John the Baptist. Then think about the modern-day prophetic voices, like Pastor Youcef Nadarkhani, who spent almost three years in an Iranian prison on blasphemy charges for preaching in the name of Christ.

I understand that persecution is relative, and I am not downplaying what you might be going through. I understand what it feels like when people work to destroy your character and strip you of your ministry. But when you consider that prophets of old were imprisoned or beheaded for their faithfulness, you can choose to see the situation as God sees it, rise above it and let the persecution make you stronger, not weaker.

Paul put it this way:

The Spirit Himself bears witness with our spirit that we are children of God, and if children, then heirs—heirs of God and joint heirs with Christ, if indeed we suffer with Him, that we may also be glorified together. For I consider that the sufferings of this present time are not worthy to be compared with the glory which shall be revealed in us.

Romans 8:16–18

Will Persecution Make You or Break You?

Although every prophet should walk meekly in a state of "bro-kenness," you should not allow persecution to break your spirit. How do you let the persecution make you and not break you?

The first step in letting persecution make you is this: Rather than looking at persecution as an opportunity to sharpen your spiritual warfare skills, look at persecution as an opportunity to become more Christlike. That is where you will find the blessing.

If anyone understands persecution, Christ does. He was mocked and spat upon. Some accused Him of having a devil. He was rejected and lied about. He was crucified. Remember, when people are persecuting you for doing the will of God, they are really persecuting Jesus. Jesus sees it; He understands it; He will repay. He will vindicate you. In the meantime, it is your job to honor Christ in the midst of the persecution.

The second step is to reflect upon your actions. When I get nasty letters from readers or see lies being written about me on the Internet, I cannot simply dismiss it as nonsense. One of my early mentors told me that there is often a grain of truth in every accusation: Look for the grain. When I get angry letters, I have to ask myself if my article was too harsh, or if it took a self-righteous turn or misinterpreted Scripture. Persecution gives me an opportunity to refine my message and grow in wisdom. But I also know that even if I am too strong in my writing, God does not condemn me, because my heart motivation is pure: to stand up for righteousness. God will vindicate me. In the meantime, I grow in grace.

The third step in letting persecution make you is to rejoice. Jesus and Paul both prophesied that persecution will come, so when it comes take Peter's advice:

> Beloved, do not think it strange concerning the fiery trial which is to try you, as though some strange thing happened to you;

124

but rejoice to the extent that you partake of Christ's sufferings, that when His glory is revealed, you may also be glad with exceeding joy.

1 Peter 4:12–13

Yes, rejoice in the midst of your persecution. This is a pattern in Scripture that you will do well to walk in. Rejoicing in persecution honors Christ, and it puts your perspective where it should be: on God.

You may be tempted to blame God for the persecution or question why He is allowing these terrible things to happen to you. Thus, the next step is this: Realize that that is always the wrong perspective. Part of the reason you are suffering this persecution is because He counts you faithful. He knows you can handle it. He knows it will make you more like Jesus. Paul wrote:

No temptation has overtaken you except such as is common to man; but God is faithful, who will not allow you to be tempted beyond what you are able, but with the temptation will also make the way of escape, that you may be able to bear it.

1 Corinthians 10:13

Nothing can separate you from the love of Christ, not even persecution (see Romans 8:35–37).

When you face persecution, honor Christ in your heart and your heart will become more Christlike. You can glory in tribulations, knowing that tribulation produces perseverance, and perseverance character, and character hope (see Romans 5:3–5). Peter wrote:

But even if you should suffer for righteousness' sake, you are blessed. "And do not be afraid of their threats, nor be troubled." But sanctify the Lord God in your hearts, and always be ready to give a defense to everyone who asks you a reason for the hope that is in you, with meekness and fear; having a good conscience, that when they defame you as evildoers, those who revile your good conduct in Christ may be ashamed.

1 Peter 3:14–16

And, the final step, turn to prayer. Jesus commands:

"You have heard that it was said, 'You shall love your neighbor and hate your enemy.' But I say to you, love your enemies, bless those who curse you, do good to those who hate you, and pray for those who spitefully use you and persecute you, that you may be sons of your Father in heaven; for He makes His sun rise on the evil and on the good, and sends rain on the just and on the unjust."

Matthew 5:43–45

Do you want a stronger prophetic anointing? Handle the persecution God's way. We never see Jesus complaining about the Pharisees and the Sadducees or the unbelievers who persecuted Him. He did not go around Samaria trashing His persecutors. He believed that God would vindicate Him—and God did.

God will do the same for you if you handle persecution His way. Look at Peter's prophetic promise: "If you are reproached for the name of Christ, blessed are you, for the Spirit of glory and of God rests upon you" (1 Peter 4:14). Amen.

17

The Battle Against Sexual Immorality

Prophetic camps in the Body of Christ were stunned when Paul Cain admitted to a pattern of homosexuality. Widely considered one of the most accurate New Testament prophets for decades—and heavily involved in the Voice of Healing revivals in the 1950s—Cain initially denied charges of homosexual behavior before finally revealing the truth.

In a written apology, Cain said: "I have struggled with homosexuality for an extended period of time. I have struggled with alcoholism for an extended period of time. I apologize for denying these matters of truth, rather than readily admitting them. I am ashamed of what I have done to hurt those close to me and for the pain I have caused those who have believed in my ministry."

Cain is not the only prophet to fall to sexual immorality—he is just one of the most visible examples in our time, and one of the few who admitted his improprieties publicly. Sexual immorality has been pursuing—and overcoming—prophets since Old Testament times. Even King David (the one God called a man after His own heart) and Solomon (the wisest man ever to live) fell prey to sexual immorality.

Sexual immorality will certainly come knocking on your door—probably more than once. There is perhaps no greater way to discredit a prophetic gifting than to entice the vessel into sexual immorality. Do not dismiss this evil assignment as irrelevant simply because you are faithfully married or single and celibate or young or old. The spirit of Jezebel is working actively to seduce prophets into immoral behaviors. Understanding Jezebel's assignment puts you in a good position to overcome it.

Warning: Jezebel Wants to Seduce You

The spirit of Jezebel works to cut off the prophetic voice any way it can—preferably by murder. Queen Jezebel massacred the prophets of the Lord in her day because they refused to compromise God's Law (see 1 Kings 18:4). Today, Jezebel seeks to murder your reputation by leading you into sin and then exposing it. That is correct. The same devil that tempts you into sexual sin wants to use that sin to destroy your ministry.

Even if your sin is not exposed, we know that "the wages of sin is death" (Romans 6:23). Be not deceived: Fornicators and adulterers will not inherit the Kingdom of God (see 1 Corinthians 6:9–10). In fact, the sexually immoral will find a place in the fiery lake of burning sulfur if they do not change their ways (see Revelation 21:8). Unrepentant sexual immorality is deadly. If you are living an immoral lifestyle, repent now because if you do not, your sin will eventually find you out (see Numbers 32:23).

When Jesus addressed the seven churches, as recorded in the book of Revelation, He praised the church at Thyatira for its works, love, service, faith and patience. But Jesus still had a few things against the leadership of this local church:

> "You allow that woman Jezebel, who calls herself a prophetess, to teach and seduce My servants to commit sexual immorality

128

and eat things sacrificed to idols. And I gave her time to repent of her sexual immorality, and she did not repent. Indeed I will cast her into a sickbed, and those who commit adultery with her into great tribulation, unless they repent of their deeds."

Revelation 2:20–22

Jezebel works to seduce prophets into sexual immorality and idolatry. Sexual immorality is any sexual act outside the covenant of marriage. That includes pornography, phone sex, masturbation, oral sex. . . . Need I go on? If the sexual encounter is not within the confines of the marriage covenant, it falls under the umbrella of sexual immorality—and it is potentially deadly.

The Bible gives warning after warning about sexual immorality. Paul told the church at Corinth to flee sexual immorality: "Every sin that a man does is outside the body," he said, "but he who commits sexual immorality sins against his own body" (1 Corinthians 6:18). Moreover, "the body is not for sexual immorality but for the Lord, and the Lord for the body" (1 Corinthians 6:13). Paul also instructed the Church to put to death "fornication, uncleanness, passion, evil desire, and covetousness, which is idolatry" (Colossians 3:5). Fornication is listed as a work of the flesh (see Galatians 5:19), and Peter begs us to abstain from fleshly lusts that war against the soul (see 1 Peter 2:11).

Jezebel will certainly come knocking on the prophet's door. The question is, What will you do when confronted with the opportunity to commit sexual sin?

Jezebel's Sexual Temptations

The battle against sexual immorality is not necessarily part of the making process, but it is indeed something many prophets face in the midst of the making. That, again, is because sex scandals—whether public or private—are one of Jezebel's most effective strategies for shutting off the prophetic voice. Jezebel pins a scarlet letter on the chest of those who fall into sexual sin, either through public exposure that leads to discrediting them or through private condemnation that causes even repentant prophets to stay hidden in caves.

Take a page from Satan's strategy to tempt Jesus in the wilderness when He was hungry: Jezebel comes to tempt you when you are in a vulnerable position. This spirit will look for any inroads it can find to seduce you. Suppose, for instance, you are married, but feel misunderstood in your prophetic walk. Or suppose you are single and going through a lonely wilderness time. Or you are discouraged in the midst of warfare, and feel like giving up. During those seasons, Jezebel might bring someone of the opposite sex into your life who seems to understand you like no one else, someone who is able to encourage you. You might not realize that Jezebel's puppets usually have hidden struggles with lust and are not coming to you with pure motives. If you form a soul tie with a lustful encourager, you could be on the path to immoral encounters.

In other words, Jezebel cannot force you into sexual immorality—but it can tempt you mightily; remember that your own carnal nature is a force to be reckoned with. This is one reason why wisdom dictates great care in spending time with and discussing personal issues with members of the opposite sex.

Be sober and vigilant because Jezebel pays close attention to the prophet and is looking for ways to devour your ministry. For more on this topic, check out my book *The Spiritual Warrior's Guide to Defeating Jezebel* (Chosen, 2013).

Renouncing Common Ground

During the making process, it is vital to renounce any common ground with Jezebel.

Ask the Holy Spirit to show you any inroads Jezebel has into your soul so you can truly walk away from the demon-inspired

130

behavior patterns that could be leading you to an immoral encounter.

Jesus said Satan had no place in Him (see John 14:30). Beyond your flesh, which you have to crucify daily, what could possibly be in you that would allow Jezebel to lead you into sexual immorality? How could Jezebel find a way to get her hooks into your soul? Take some time right now to explore this topic with the Holy Spirit.

If you have issues with lust, Jezebel already has her hooks in you. Jesus said if a man even looks at a woman with lust he has already committed adultery with her in his heart (see Matthew 5:28). And the same holds true for women who look at men with lust in their hearts. Although we are in a dispensation of grace and no longer under the Law, the seventh commandment— "Thou shalt not commit adultery" (Exodus 20:14 KJV)—is still God's order for sexual purity.

Abstaining from Fleshly Lusts

If Jezebel cannot silence your voice, it is satisfied to leave you hiding in a cave of obscurity where no one can hear—and perhaps no one wants to hear—what you have to say. Prophets trapped in Jezebel's deadly web of sexual immorality tend to have one of three responses: they wallow in guilt and condemnation; they deceive themselves and continue in sin; or they repent and allow the Holy Spirit to restore them. Prophets who lick their self-inflicted wounds in the cave of condemnation become silent. Prophets who continue sinning are eventually exposed and discredited. Either way, Jezebel wins. Repentance can bring restoration, of course, but it is far better not to fall into Jezebel's trap at all.

Again, Peter begged us—as sojourners and pilgrims—to abstain from fleshly lusts that war against the soul (see 1 Peter 2:11). Those fleshly lusts are not limited to sexual immorality— but sexual immorality defiles you. Jesus said it is not what comes out of a man that defiles him, but, rather, the evil things that come from within bring defilement (see Mark 7:18–23). Jesus listed adulteries, fornication and lewdness (being sexually unchaste) among the defiling influences in a person's heart. In other words: sexual immorality. God's will is our sanctification—that we should abstain from sexual immorality and learn how to possess our vessels with honor (see 1 Thessalonians 4:3–5).

So how can you abstain from fleshly lusts during your making process? Much the same way you overcome any sin.

First, avoid situations that could expose you to temptation. As I mentioned above, take care how you spend time alone with members of the opposite sex. If you struggle with same-sex attraction, do not be alone with members of the same sex.

Second, if you find yourself being tempted to indulge in sexual sin, walk away from it. Walking away is submitting yourself to God because His Word warns us to flee sexual immorality (see 1 Corinthians 6:18) and youthful lusts (see 2 Timothy 2:22). The Bible says that if we submit to God and resist the devil he will flee (see James 4:7).

It is no great mystery, really. If you are being tempted sexually because you allowed yourself to be put into such a position—if you could have avoided the temptation in the first place but failed to do so—you still have the opportunity to flee before falling into sin. Flee and flee fast.

The temptation to sin is not a sin. But if your imaginations are running wild and you feel you are going to lose the fight against the spirit of immorality, confess your weakness and get prayer immediately. James said: "Confess your trespasses to one another, and pray for one another, that you may be healed" (James 5:16). And he added that the effective, fervent prayer of a righteous person makes tremendous power available.

If you continue struggling with lustful temptations that you cannot seem to shake, seek counsel. Do not try to fight the battle alone.

If you have already fallen into sin, the same rule applies. Confess it to a mature brother or sister, and get counsel and prayer. Repent for putting yourself in that situation and set your heart not to repeat that mistake. Then get back up and fight again.

Third, after you have fled, pursue righteous living, faithfulness, love and peace with brothers and sisters in Christ who call on the Lord with pure hearts (see 2 Timothy 2:22). In other words, seek God and surround yourself with people who are also going hard after Him. Ask God for help in overcoming temptations toward sexual immorality, renew your mind with the Word of God and learn to cast down unholy imaginations. When you walk with the Holy Spirit, you will not do what your sinful nature craves (see Galatians 5:16).

It is possible that a spirit of lust could be oppressing you and deliverance might be the appropriate solution. But if you do not go hard after God in the wake of deliverance—if you do not renew your mind, stay filled with the Holy Spirit and minister to the Lord—you could wind up worse. Remember what Jesus said:

"When an unclean spirit goes out of a man, he goes through dry places, seeking rest; and finding none, he says, 'I will return to my house from which I came.' And when he comes, he finds it swept and put in order. Then he goes and takes with him seven other spirits more wicked than himself, and they enter and dwell there; and the last state of that man is worse than the first."

Luke 11:24–26

Sexual temptation is nothing to play with—and neither is deliverance. If you are battling sexual immorality, get help. This is the domain of Jezebel, and going to war with this principality without backup has destroyed too many lives and ministries.

Again, if you are struggling with lust, reach out and seek ministry before you fall into sin. And if you have already fallen, reach out and seek the ministry of restoration. God can still use you if you have truly repented. If you doubt that, read about the life of King David. He fell into sexual immorality, but he kept his kingship.

18

Living Victoriously in Warfare

It was one thing after another. At least, at that point, I was able to sit up and talk with a friend while trying to swallow solid food after catching a violent virus my daughter brought home from the mission field. That was the fifth time in eight months I had been hit with sickness.

Just a week before, I had heard news so devastating that I had had little choice but to trade sleep for prayer just to maintain. And the week before that someone in my inner circle launched a verbal attack against me that left me wondering how I had misjudged his character so badly.

I could go on about this fourteen-day period when it seemed all hell was breaking loose against me. Call it a season of spiritual warfare. Call it a trial. Call it tribulation. It would not be the first time I had endured waves of spiritual attack, and I knew it would not be the last.

But I started wondering: Does everyone get assaulted like this, or was I doing something wrong? It was a question that had haunted me for years. I am not practicing sin. I do not have demonic icons in my house. I pray and study the Word. I am not perfect, but I am going after God. Although it is not wise to compare, it seems that I get a lot more spiritual whacks upside the head than my friends.

I came to learn that it is all part of walking in the prophetic.

Prophets must weather heavy seasons of spiritual warfare. Some warfare manifestations are merely annoying time stealers or pesky thorns in the flesh. But there are major spiritual attacks that can, at times, blindside you. As you begin to comprehend the enemy's disdain for the prophetic anointing and learn to see the realm of the spirit through God-colored glasses, you will be better prepared to respond to the onslaught when it comes—and it will come.

Prophetic Advice from an Apostolic Mentor

After years of pondering the question *Does everybody get this much spiritual warfare?* and not really coming up with much more than teaching on "fiery trials," I spoke with an apostolic mentor who helped open my eyes. I had already examined myself—but anyone can be deceived. If there was anything I could do differently to avoid the onslaughts—some of which were near-deadly—then I wanted to make a swift adjustment. I needed someone who had the insight to see what I could not see.

My apostolic mentor offered me these six words: *Warfare goes along with prophetic ministry.* I knew this already, of course. I taught it. I wrote about it. I counseled regarding it. But for some reason there was a disconnect between what I understood and how I walked it out. I had the revelation, but I had lost the practical application to my life. That day it "clicked." As the discussion continued, my mentor said: "You'll have to settle in your mind that your gift causes warfare—and that it could well have an impact on the people around you."

I have witnessed that truth many times over the years. On the one hand, the prophetic anointing on your life can cause people with unresolved emotional or spiritual issues to manifest them with anger or control or some other ungodly behavior when they are with you. People are drawn to prophets, but if their motives are not pure—or if they need deliverance from oppressive spirits—the prophetic anointing exposes it so it can be dealt with.

On the other hand, the prophetic anointing stirs up devils that can attack your friends, family or church simply by association. The devil has gone after my daughter numerous times. My graphic designer jokes that he is going to add an extra fee for the witchcraft that hits him when he works on my projects. And when I accepted the position of executive pastor of a local church, we came under heavy attack immediately: There were two attempted break-ins, the landlord began complaining about the homeless people we served and attendance dropped off dramatically in the first month.

It can be frustrating, but I had to learn to accept the fact that with all the upsides of the prophetic gifting, there is a downside: intense spiritual warfare. You have undoubtedly received teaching about the "plus and minus" sides of the cross for the believer. The plus side is all the blessings—redemption, grace, peace, etc. The minus side is the hardships and trials that believers generally want to avoid.

The Body of Christ today is leaning toward the plus side of the cross while backing away from the disciplines such as prayer and fasting. Churches present a "seeker-friendly" gospel or some other ear-tickling, soul-pleasing church experience. The pure prophetic word brings the reality of the cross—the truth. The devil hates it and many Christians do not like it, either. If you are walking as an uncompromising prophet, that makes you a target.

"I Bring Warfare"

Prophets are desperately needed at this hour in Church history, so it should not come as any surprise that the warfare is increasing.

Watch that you are not taken off guard by the sometimes unpleasant consequences of operating in your prophetic ministry. The signs and wonders of a prophet—such as prophesying, breaking things open in the spirit and casting out demons—are following you. That stirs up devils. Walk with both eyes open, seeing things from a natural and spiritual perspective.

The negative manifestations that arise in your midst are not negative to God—and they precede a breakthrough. Expect the warfare and condition your mind to ask God, "What do You want me to see in this situation?" Stay close to counsel. That way, if you are seeing things the wrong way or operating in your flesh someone can tell you. The minute you isolate yourself from the counsel of trusted voices in your life is the minute the devil will move in to take advantage. Keep a guard on your heart and a guard on your soul and a guard on your prayers. Stay heavily guarded and clean.

I had to recondition my mind to think *I bring warfare*. I do not actually say that to people, of course. I do not broadcast it. I do not confess it over my life in that sense, but I acknowledge it. And I am not afraid of it. I do not question it anymore. I turn to God and ask Him how He wants me to walk it out as an individual and as someone who lives, works and ministers alongside others. And I have learned to pay closer attention for the manifestation of the breakthrough—the victory.

God created you for such a time as this. This is who you are. It is not about a title. It is about walking worthy of your calling so the people God has called you to touch can break through.

When All Hell Breaks Loose Against You

So what do you do when hell breaks loose against you? That is when you have to rush back to Bible basics. The devil is ultimately after your peace and your joy. Why do you think the Bible instructs us to rejoice in trials? James said to count it all joy when we encounter trials (see James 1:2), and Peter told us not to think it strange that a fiery trial has come our way—but to rejoice (see 1 Peter 4:12). So rejoice, and understand who the enemy is. The enemy is not flesh and blood—and it is not God.

Consider Paul the apostle. He was a prisoner on a ship heading for Rome and caught in a great storm. He was hungry from fasting. Nevertheless, he remained an encouragement to those around him—even to his captors. Paul continued to stand on God's Word—"I believe God that it will be just as it was told me"—that they would all reach shore safely even though the ship would be lost (Acts 27:22–25). That is spiritual maturity.

When the ship was wrecked, the soldiers planned to kill all the prisoners so that none could swim away and escape. The centurion wanted to save Paul, however, and commanded that all on the ship make their way to shore by swimming or floating on boards or planks. It turned out just as Paul had said: They all reached land safely. And when a viper bit Paul, he did not have a panic attack for fear that he was about to die. Instead, he continued to stand on God's word that he would reach Rome alive (see verse 24). He kept believing God that it would be just as it was told him.

That must be our response when it feels as though all hell is breaking loose against us. We have to go back to the Word—even if we have to get a concordance and look for Scriptures that may relate to the specific trial—and find out what God has to say about the situation. Then we should believe God that it will be just as it was told to us. And we should seriously rejoice, because when all hell breaks loose against us we can rest assured that all of heaven covers our backs. We war from a place of victory.

What If Your Battle Was Already Won?

I remember when I battled for my first piece of property, a condominium. It is a long story, but here is the short version.

I was scheduled to leave for a mission trip to Latin America and had to delay the closing. The timing was terrible. But while I was on the mission field, the Lord gave me a "rhema" word. I was sitting there and I heard the Spirit of God say: *Jeremiah 32:10*. I had no idea what Jeremiah 32:10 said, so I got up and fetched my Bible. It says this: "I signed the deed and sealed it, called witnesses, and weighed out for him the money on the scales" (Jeremiah 32:10 AMPLIFIED).

When I read that Scripture, it struck my spirit. And then God told me not to worry. That was enough for me. That was the Lord's way of assuring me that He had my purchase of the property all under control. I accepted that word as true and waited to see what would transpire.

Well, when I returned, all hell broke loose. First, my loan fell through. By God's grace, the seller's agent allowed me to go ahead and move into the condo while the mortgage broker arranged another loan. Because I had that prophetic word from the Lord that the deal was in effect "signed and sealed," I started renovating the place. I got a new oven and some other new appliances. I had contractors start installing a wood floor.

Then I got more bad news: The second loan had fallen through. It happened because the broker had not accommodated some portion of the real estate law. The loan was denied two more times in the course of the next six weeks.

In the midst of the financial challenge, the seller, who was Russian and a Mafioso type, lost patience with the arrangement we had agreed upon. He tried to steal my keys. He confronted me in the hallway with rage in his eyes and profanity in his mouth. He banged on my door morning, noon and night, sent threats and otherwise worked to intimidate me. Even my agent felt I should give up. I held tight—and I held on to Jeremiah 32:10.

Once during the heat of the battle, the Lord asked me how I would be acting if the war was already won. I knew, of course, that I would be rejoicing and thanking Him. That is our battle stance no matter what stage of the war we find ourselves in. No matter what type of warfare the prophet is facing when standing on God's word, we know that Jesus already overcame the world so we can be of good cheer. We cannot whine about the spiritual warfare. We have to rise above it. We are seated in heavenly places in Christ Jesus. We wage war from a place of victory.

Jeremiah 32:10 turned out to be a true rhema word from God. Not only did I close on the condo, but I found out something at the closing table that made my jaw drop. For all the ranting and raving the Russian Mafioso did, for all the threatening and intimidation . . . he had actually signed the title deed over to me while I was in Latin America nearly two months earlier. The deed giving me ownership of the property was signed and sealed long before the loan went through. And it gets even better. My Realtor paid the mortgage for the first six weeks I was in the condo before it closed. Hallelujah!

Why so much spiritual warfare? Because the devil hates the prophetic voice. But we have victory in Christ. Our job is to submit ourselves to God, exercise the authority of the believer, resist the devil and rejoice in the finished work of the cross.

19

Coming to Forks in the Road

When I was in high school I enjoyed poetry. One of my favorite poems was Robert Frost's "The Road Not Taken." It talks about a fork in the road in the woods. The writer wants to travel both roads but has to choose one—and he realizes he will likely never have an opportunity to explore the other. He ponders which road to take for some time, weighing the pros and cons of each. In the end, he takes the road "less traveled by" and declares "that has made all the difference."

At some point in your prophetic ministry—and likely at different points along your journey—you will meet with a fork in the road. The Holy Spirit will lead and guide you, but ultimately you have a free will and can choose which path to take. One path may look more attractive than the other. One path may be more difficult than the other. Make no mistake, the road you choose to take does make all the difference. I urge you to take the road less traveled by. This is biblical advice: Jesus advised us to enter through the narrow gate (see Matthew 7:13–14). The gate is wide that leads to destruction, and that is the way many prophets go. Take the narrow path.

A fork in the road always demands a decision, and it is often a difficult decision to make. I find that there are three particular challenges prophets are likely to face in this regard. Your fork in the road might require you to stay the course, when you want to take the easier route of giving up. Your fork in the road might require you to leave, when you want to stay on that comfortable path. Your fork in the road might require a decision to believe that God will equip you when you cannot imagine that you could be qualified to fulfill such a challenging assignment.

Let's look at these three types of forks in the road. Sometimes the decision to follow God is voluntary. Sometimes it comes our way unexpectedly. In other words, sometimes we have a clear view ahead and can choose our path, and sometimes life delivers events we never saw coming that force us to react as best we can. Note, however, that we do not choose the warfare.

When You Feel Like Quitting

All prophets feel like giving up at some point in their ministries—maybe more than once. Prophetic ministry is a pressure cooker. Once your ministry is known, people will constantly expect you to prophesy, and the temptation mounts to speak a word without a clear unction from the Holy Spirit. This tension gets tiring, and the spiritual warfare you will be involved in as a matter of course also can bring weariness to your soul. I cannot tell you how many times I have felt like giving up. I thank God I have persevered.

Paul knew we would feel like quitting sometimes. That is why he admonished us not to "lose heart and grow weary and faint in acting nobly and doing right, for in due time and at the appointed season we shall reap, if we do not loosen and relax our courage and faint" (Galatians 6:9 AMPLIFIED). The truth is, trials will come. The truth is, warfare will come. The truth is, temptations will come—and positive thinking and positive confessions will not stop them from coming. But here is the truth you should focus on: God loves you, and your faith pleases Him.

Satan is after your intimate relationship with Christ and your faith in Him. If you feel discouraged, stressed, overworked or ready to quit, just hang on. Everyone feels like giving up sometimes, and this usually happens when we are trying to do in our own strength what He called us to do in His. Cry out to God. He is listening. Thank God for His grace. He pours it out on the humble. And thank God that we do not have to be afraid—because He is with us and no weapon formed against us can prosper. Turn from the quitter's path. Take the soldier's path: Endure.

When You Are Too Comfortable

We can all get comfortable in ministry—sometimes too comfortable. So comfortable, in fact, that we camp out in a place God is trying to get us to leave. That happened to me. I was so comfortable in one particular ministry I vowed I would never leave. How ignorant and immature I was about God's ways! The Holy Spirit nudged me gently for years, yet I would not leave because I did not want to give up what was familiar and gratifying. Finally, God, in His mercy, made it so uncomfortable for me to stay that suddenly I could not get out of there fast enough.

It usually happens that the old thing looks more attractive than the new thing. That is where trust and obedience come in. It is vital that you follow the Holy Spirit rather than camping out in a place He has already left. If not, you could miss your prophetic destiny and fall prey to "religion." Remember, the old thing serves as a foundation for the new thing God is calling you to do—and you cannot usually do both at the same time. God might transition your ministry for reasons you cannot fathom and will only understand years later. Be assured He "works all things according to the counsel of His will" (Ephesians 1:11).

Andrew was one of the first of John's disciples to catch on to what the Spirit was doing in his day. Here is the scene: John the Baptist was standing with Andrew and another of his disciples when Jesus walked by. John said, "Behold the Lamb of God!" (John 1:36 KJV). Those two disciples heard John, and they followed Jesus immediately. Andrew quickly fetched his brother, Simon Peter, and told him they had found the Messiah. From there, the movement began to gain momentum. Philip and Nathanael joined the revolution next, and others soon followed until there were multitudes.

Not all of John's disciples followed the Spirit, though, and some of them got religious. Remember when Jesus and John were both baptizing? John's disciples were none too happy. They went to him and whined, "Rabbi, you know the one who was with you on the other side of the Jordan? The one you authorized with your witness? Well, he's now competing with us. He's baptizing, too, and everyone's going to him instead of us" (John 3:26 MESSAGE).

What about you, prophet? Are you holding on to a past move that has dried up? Or are you moving with God daily as He continues to reveal His plans and His ways? Ask God to show you if you have some catching up to do. It is never too late to follow the Spirit out of those dry places. *The Message* puts it this way: "Forget about what's happened; don't keep going over old history. Be alert, be present. I'm about to do something brand-new. It's bursting out! Don't you see it? There it is! I'm making a road through the desert, rivers in the badlands" (Isaiah 43:18–19). Follow the river of God's Living Water.

When You Feel Underqualified

God never asks you to do something you cannot achieve, but He will stretch you further than you may think you can go. Kingdom promotions are exciting. There was a two-year period of my life where I saw promotion after promotion after promotion. But with promotion comes more responsibility—and it can get overwhelming if you lose the right perspective.

After a season of stripping—you may call it the dark night of the soul—followed by a season of rest, God started a restoration process in my life that is beyond anything my eyes could have seen or my ears could have heard. I often joke now that the proverbial one-armed paperhanger has an advantage on me. In other words, the current ministries God has called me to—from editing to leadership to pastoring to writing—generate so much pressure they could easily overwhelm me if I let them.

When God calls you to a new assignment, a sense of being overwhelmed often follows the initial excitement. You have a choice: Believe God, or allow the enemy to come in like a flood. When God called me into prophetic ministry, He told me, *Think back to the petitions you have made of Me and this won't seem so overwhelming. You showed yourself willing. I will make you able. Lean and depend on Me and not on your own understanding. Thus do the prophets.*

When God calls you to a new assignment, think about the years you cried out for God to use you. This new assignment is one of His answers. You are at a fork in the road. You can accept it and glorify God—you can say, "Here am I! Send me" (Isaiah 6:8)—or you can tell God all the reasons why you are not qualified and refuse to take on what He is asking you to do. I can assure you, great rewards await obedience. Yes, there will be pressure, but if you trust in the Lord He will walk you through it and you will gain strength.

What Now?

You will face various other forks in the road along your journey. Some decisions will seem harder than others. We have talked, for instance, about the crucial decision to maintain a lifestyle of holiness when you are tempted to slip onto the inviting path to sin. Sometimes following God will meet with the disapproval of people close to you. Other times, following God will bring accusations that you have missed His heart—or even that you are being deceived (the subject of our next chapter).

Take courage in the fact that if you acknowledge God in everything, He will show you which path to take (see Proverbs 3:6). If you seek God with your whole heart at any given fork in the road, you will find Him (see Deuteronomy 4:29). He is not trying to hide His will from you. Most likely, He will lead you on the path less traveled by. And when you obey, it will make all the difference.

20

Avoiding Spiritual Deception

I was deceived. I did not know it at the time, of course. That is one of the problems with deception. You never know you are deceived until the Holy Spirit breaks in and shows you the truth. Usually, that breakthrough comes in the wake of your growing sense of "dis-ease" about a situation, and finally seeking the truth even though it might be painful to hear.

Not long after I was saved, I began attending a church that taught about the fivefold ministries of Ephesians 4:11—the specific callings to the offices of apostle, prophet, evangelist, pastor and teacher. The problem was the legalism and authoritarianism with which the pastor applied this verse to his own ministry. What seemed like exciting new revelation to me, though, was really a door of deception that led to all manner of false doctrine.

I was so hungry to learn about God, I somehow failed to see that God's love was never mentioned. Rather, a workhorse mentality prized performance over passion for Jesus. People's needs were neglected for the sake of building one man's kingdom. We were rewarded for actions that built up the pastor's ministry and rebuked for actions that slowed the growth of his agenda. I was the golden child for several years—I served out of a pure heart to build the Kingdom—so I was surprised when people close to me began to question some of the teachings and demands.

I pooh-poohed it at first, but those seeds of truth eventually sprouted, and I began to see how the pastor's teaching on the fivefold ministry offices was not new revelation at all. Rather it was perverted doctrine designed to establish his position over us and control us with fear. But there is no fear in love. Perfect love drives out fear (see 1 John 4:18). I watched as many people left the church claiming that the love of Christ was not there. When they did, the pastor quickly marked them as deceived. But they were not deceived, I was—and so was the leadership.

As the evidence of the deception began piling up, I started crying out to God. I wanted to know the truth. I went to the leadership and voiced some of my concerns. I was told that the teaching was true—and that I was wrong to question it. At that point, I knew that one way or another I had fallen into deception. But which was it? Was the teaching wrong or was my mistrust of it wrong? I prayed for months for God to break the deception off my mind. Suddenly, I saw clearly. I left the church. Even then, the enemy tried to make me think I had left in error. But God has proven abundantly that it was His voice I was following.

Would You Know If You Were Deceived?

Whether you have been in prophetic ministry for decades or are just entering prophetic ministry, you can be deceived. In fact, if you do no not think you can be deceived then you are already deceived. I submit to you that we are all walking in some measure of deception. The enemy has told all of us lies that we believe about ourselves, lies that hold us back or cause us to react in an ungodly manner. If we were completely free, I believe we would be walking in much greater authority and anointing.

Deception is progressive, like Usher syndrome, a rare genetic disorder that gradually causes blindness. People do not move from worshiping God to worshiping angels overnight, for example. People do not take one giant leap from the practical study of biblical types and shadows to the practice of occultism. It starts with one of those little "foxes"—such as Solomon said spoil the vines. Just as the Word of God warns us that one sin can lead to another sin (read: David and Bathsheba), it is also true that one error can lead to another error. One wrong belief can cause us to believe many wrong things.

The devil first has to seduce us before he can deceive us, and he will usually start with something that seems on the up and up. After all, the apostle Paul warned us that Satan transforms himself into an angel of light (see 2 Corinthians 11:14). But considering all the warnings in Scripture about deceiving spirits, how does deception get its stronghold? Well, one way is ignorance of the Word of God and the ways of God. But deception also finds a doorway in the idolatry of our hearts.

The Bible says that "the heart is deceitful above all things, and desperately wicked" (Jeremiah 17:9). If that is true, and it is, then none of us is above deception. If we think we are, as I said, we are deceived already. The good news is Jesus sent the Holy Ghost to lead and guide us into all truth—truth that is readily confirmed in the canon of Scripture. If we follow His Spirit and His written Word instead of the idolatry of our hearts, we will walk in the light.

Idolatry's Slippery Slope

Idolatry is always a danger. The apostle Paul lists it as a work of the flesh (see Galatians 5:20). But the same apostle, under the same Holy Spirit inspiration, also told us to flee from idolatry (see 1 Corinthians 10:14). The Word of God never instructs us to do something the grace of God will not empower us to do. We simply have to get into agreement.

Noteworthy is a comparison between two verses that deal with *fleeing*. The Bible implores us to submit ourselves to God and resist the devil, for then the devil will flee from us (see James 4:7). But the Bible does not say that idolatry will flee from us. Rather, it says we have to flee from idolatry. Why?

Any time we seek our own will instead of God's will—whenever our hearts turn inward—we are standing on the threshold of idolatry. The tempter wastes no time in slipping a toe in the door and soon gains entry. Consider Paul's warning:

> Therefore, my dearly beloved, shun (keep clear away from, avoid by flight if need be) any sort of idolatry (of loving or venerating anything more than God). I am speaking as to intelligent (sensible) men. Think over and make up your minds [for yourselves] about what I say. [I appeal to your reason and your discernment in these matters.]
>
> 1 Corinthians 10:14–15 AMPLIFIED

We cannot blame all this deception business on the devil. Nor can we be ignorant of his devices. Part of his work is to find the idolatry in our hearts: the deceitfulness of riches, the pride of life, the lust of the flesh or something else that causes us to give God's place to another. Once Satan finds that idolatry he will tempt us with it. At that point we have a clear choice: Destroy the idol or walk into darkness.

Guard Your Heart

We should partner with the Lord in guarding our hearts with all diligence from deception in these last days. Most of us would never consider turning to occultic practices to discover hidden meanings and call it prophetic ministry. Likewise, most of us would never exalt angels to a place they do not deserve—or even want. And most of us would never offer "strange fire" in the name of Jesus. Strange fire is often introduced when we mix other religious philosophies into Christianity, like New Age or Kabbalah. It promotes elements beyond the boundaries of Scripture in the name of the Lord.

Yet some have fallen into these snares. We see these things happening in the Body of Christ even now.

Again, deception is progressive. It starts with those little foxes. Guarding our hearts from deception means being humble enough to acknowledge that we are capable of being deceived. It also means setting our minds on Christ and putting first the Kingdom. As far as the world is concerned, we have died, and our real life is hidden with Christ in God (see Colossians 3:3). Guarding ourselves from deception, then, means taking the apostle Paul's advice:

> Kill (deaden, deprive of power) the evil desire lurking in your members [those animal impulses and all that is earthly in you that is employed in sin]: sexual vice, impurity, sensual appetites, unholy desires, and all greed and covetousness, for that is idolatry (the deifying of self and other created things instead of God).
>
> Colossians 3:5 AMPLIFIED

Prophets are called to holiness and humility. We should be turning our hearts away from sin and toward God—not mysticism, angels or anything else. We have watched some in prophetic ministry stray from its purpose, sometimes actually through the effort of trying not to appear "religious." Yes, we want to make room for God to move however He desires, and we want to avoid the trap of a religious spirit that would quench His operations. But does that mean we throw our discernment out stained-glass windows in order to prove we are open-minded? God forbid.

Falling into Prophetic Deception

Many books have been written and many sermons have been preached about avoiding spiritual deception, but that has not kept prophets from falling into the devil's traps. The enemy roams about like a roaring lion seeking prophets to devour. There were two Old Testament prophets who actually faced lions. One walked away. The other was devoured. Both were essentially dealing with idolatry in the land. But one obeyed unto life and the other disobeyed unto death.

In 1 Kings 13, we read the story of the latter of these two prophets. God confirmed the prophecy of this unnamed young man with a sign (King Jeroboam's hand was withered and restored), and he left for his next assignment. That is when the young prophet met up with an old prophet named Bethel who invited him back to his home for dinner. The young prophet told him, "I cannot return with you nor go in with you; neither can I eat bread nor drink water with you in this place. For I have been told by the word of the LORD, 'You shall not eat bread nor drink water there, nor return by going the way you came'" (1 Kings 13:16).

This young prophet, though, fell into deception. The older prophet told him that an angel had spoken to him by the word of the Lord, saying, "Bring him back with you to your house, that he may eat bread and drink water" (1 Kings 13:18). That old prophet was lying to him, but the young prophet did not discern it. So he went back with the old prophet, ate bread and drank water. That is when the old prophet delivered a true and unfortunate prophecy:

> "Thus says the LORD: 'Because you have disobeyed the word of
> the LORD, and have not kept the commandment which the LORD

your God commanded you, but you came back, ate bread, and drank water in the place of which the LORD said to you, "Eat no bread and drink no water," your corpse shall not come to the tomb of your fathers.'"

1 Kings 13:21–22

As the Bible account goes, a lion met him on the road and killed him. The old prophet gathered up the young man's body for burial in his own tomb.

There are many lessons in this story. There is the lesson that just because someone more mature than you in the prophetic says something is true does not mean it is true. There is also the lesson that even a prophet who is flowing in a strong prophetic anointing with signs following can fall into deception. No mention is made that the young prophet went back to the Lord to inquire about the older prophet's word. He did not test the spirits. Ultimately, he disobeyed God and it cost him his life. Prophets will face the test of obedience over and over again during the making process. When we disobey, we open the door to deception.

How to Avoid Spiritual Deception

Daniel also faced a lion—several of them—but he came out of it alive. I believe he fared so well while exiled in Babylon—a symbol of the world's system—because he obeyed God. He was *in* the world, but not *of* the world. Obedience is the master key for avoiding spiritual deception. Daniel also offered a model for prayer that I believe is helpful in avoiding spiritual deception: Repent, pray God's will and stand your ground (see Daniel 9).

Before Daniel set out to pray for his nation, he repented. The Bible says he set his face toward God "to make request by prayer and supplications, with fasting, sackcloth, and ashes" (Daniel 9:3). When we come before the Lord in prayer, we first need to repent for our sin. If we claim we have no sin, we are deceiving ourselves before we even get started (see 1 John 1:8). We all sin by commission or omission more often than we even realize. By starting out with repentance, we are cleansed from all unrighteousness, and we have confidence in our prayer.

Next, Daniel released his prayer in faith—and with fervency. The effective, fervent prayer of a righteous person makes tremendous power available (see James 5:16). Daniel acknowledged God's character and called on His nature—not his own righteousness—as the basis for the answer to prayer he sought. Meditating on the character of God can also help us avoid spiritual deception because we will discern when something does not align with who God is. This one principle—there is no counterfeit for God's love—will take you a long way toward avoiding the enemy's snare.

Finally, Daniel stood his ground. Daniel 9:21 tells us that as part of a larger vision, he saw the angel Gabriel being dispatched to him at the beginning of his prayer and fasting. The angel did not arrive instantaneously, however, so Daniel continued to pray until the answer came.

In another time of prayer and fasting, Daniel received an angelic visitation that reveals how spiritual warfare works in the heavenlies (see Daniel 10). The angel told him that his prayer was heard the first day he released it, but that the prince of the kingdom of Persia withstood him 21 days. Michael, one of the chief princes, came to help in the spiritual battle.

Sometimes seeing answered prayer means standing your ground despite the fact that nothing appears to be changing. Angels hearken to the voice of God's word (see Psalm 103:20). Your intercession empowers the angels to war in the unseen realm.

Stay in the habit of being quick to repent, praying God's will—and God's will only—and standing your ground. And while you are at it, pray for the grace of obedience. Do you want to avoid deception and flow in a more powerful prophetic anointing? Obedience is key. Andrew Murray put it this way in his classic *The Spirit of Christ*:

> Let us cry to God very earnestly, that He may waken His Church and people to take in this double lesson: A living obedience is indispensable to the full experience of the indwelling; the full experience of the indwelling is what a loving obedience may certainly claim. Let each of us even now say to our Lord that we do love Him, and keep His commandments. In however much feebleness and failure it be, still let us speak it out to Him as the one purpose of our souls; this He will accept. Let us believe in the indwelling of the Spirit as already given to us, when in the obedience of faith we gave ourselves to Him. Let us believe that the full indwelling, with the revelation of Christ within, can be ours. And let us be content with nothing less than the loving, reverent, trembling, but blessed consciousness that we are the Temples of the Living God, because the Spirit of God dwelleth in us.

21

Becoming One with Your Message

I am looking at a tattered, water-stained piece of paper on which I long ago typed out a message the Lord gave me—for me. It was essentially an exhortation calling me to serve as a messenger in His Kingdom. At the time, I had no idea how prophetic ministry operated or how it would manifest in messages.

Soon, I would discover that I had a "watchman" calling. As I explained in chapter 4, the watchman tends to receive warnings and messages given to set the captives free from deception—or prevent them from falling into the enemy's trap. It is not the most popular prophetic mantle to carry; nor is it usually easy to walk out. I stumbled through many trials and tribulations in order to develop the passion I needed to sound the alarm of truth in love.

You might say I had to become one with my message. I had to learn from my own mistakes. I had to break free from various forms of bondage and deception. I had to endure spiritual abuse. I had to suffer being stripped of my ministry so that I could carry the ministry He called me to. I had to learn that I could not build a prophetic ministry on my writing gift—I had to yield my writing gift to help move His prophetic purposes forward. Above all, I had to learn to put my confidence fully in Christ and Christ alone.

Like John the Baptist, you must decrease as a prophet so that Jesus can increase in your ministry (see John 3:30). That is quite the opposite of what we see in today's glamorized prophetic movement. Prophetic prima donnas preach the same hyped-up message across the circuit without passionately pursuing the truth they swear by. Popularity has become the measure of success for some prophets. But make no mistake: Boldly preaching what you are not actively pursuing is hypocrisy.

In order to sustain a true prophetic ministry over decades you need to maintain passion for the message the Lord has called you to carry. You need to become one with the message. True prophets become one with their messages through humbling encounters with God, man and the devil. It is part of the making process that never stops.

Keeping the Right Perspective

I want to mention here that there is a lot of talk in prophetic circles today about modern-day schools for prophets—equipping centers where individuals can be trained for prophetic ministry. Equipping prophetic voices is vital in the last days. But sometimes the training fails to distinguish between the office of prophet and the gifting, a distinction we have discussed. Sometimes, as well, immature Christians decide on their own that they are called to the prophetic office and are misled in their callings. It is easy to pay an online school, complete a few worksheets and receive a certificate of ordination as a prophet. This is dangerous for them and can damage the credibility of the true prophet.

It is important to remember that Samuel's school of the prophets was not producing Elijahs or Elishas—nor was it intended to. Samuel's school of the prophets produced what you might call scholastic prophets trained in Scripture. These prophets had the task of the recording or chronicling various events. They did not carry the same calling or anointing as those God used to call down fire from heaven, raise the dead or prophesy to kings.

Prophetic ministry is not something someone does at church on Sunday—like a weekend warrior who bungee jumps or climbs mountains. Nor is it something a person can choose to become. For true prophets, prophetic ministry is not what they do; it is who they are. In other words, true prophets become one with their messages.

Seeing Yourself in Scripture

Your life should be a letter anyone can read. Put another way, it should be apparent that you have actually walked out—or are actively walking out—the prophetic message you are carrying. Often, you become one with your message in wilderness places. In the wilderness, God molds you in dramatic fashion so He can unveil you at the appointed time with a revelation that you refuse to compromise because it has become part of your reality.

John the Baptist, again, is our example. John came boldly proclaiming a message of repentance and prophesying the soon-coming Messiah. John saw himself in Scripture. He knew who he was—a voice crying in the wilderness to make straight the way of the Lord—and he declared it (see John 1:23). During his wilderness experience, John became one with his message. When he emerged, he fulfilled his mission to prepare the people for Christ's coming.

Jesus later said of John:

> "Who is this man in the wilderness that you went out to see? Did you find him weak as a reed, moved by every breath of wind? Or

159

were you expecting to see a man dressed in expensive clothes? Those who dress like that live in palaces, not out in the wilderness. Were you looking for a prophet? Yes, and he is more than a prophet. John is the man to whom the Scriptures refer when they say, 'Look, I am sending my messenger before you, and he will prepare your way before you.' I assure you, of all who have ever lived, none is greater than John the Baptist."

Matthew 11:7–10 NLT

What a testimony from Jesus!

Can you see yourself in Scripture? Malachi might not have prophesied about your coming on to the scene, but maybe you can relate to one of the prophets in the Bible. Maybe you recognize some of the markings of Isaiah or Moses or Hosea in your ministry. Maybe you have a similar mandate as an Old Testament counterpart who spoke of deliverance or prayer or dreams or warnings or miracles. Although there are key differences between New Testament and Old Testament prophets, there are also key similarities. As you work with the Lord to become one with your message, take encouragement from those who have gone before you and how they stood for God in the face of impossibilities.

Have You Eaten the Scroll?

God used Ezekiel in ways that would make most of us cringe. Ezekiel used prophetic demonstrations over and over again to send a message of warning to Israel—and sometimes those prophetic demonstrations came at a great discomfort. This was part of Ezekiel becoming one with his message. It began with the Lord telling him to eat a scroll, then go and give its message to Israel (see Ezekiel 3).

After Ezekiel ate the scroll, the Lord told him: "Son of man, receive into your heart all My words that I speak to you, and hear with your ears" (Ezekiel 3:10). The New Living Translation of this verse reads: "Son of man, let all my words sink deep into your own heart first. Listen to them carefully for yourself." And *The Message* puts it this way: "Son of man, get all these words that I'm giving you inside you. Listen to them obediently. Make them your own." In other words, become one with the message.

Soon, God told Ezekiel to place the sins of Israel upon himself. God instructed Ezekiel to do this by lying on his left side for 390 days—one day for each year of the nation's sin. After that, Ezekiel was commanded to lie on his right side for forty days—one day for each year of Judah's sin (see Ezekiel 4:1–6). While lying on his side, Ezekiel was told to prophesy Israel's destruction. The Lord actually tied him up in some manner so that he would not be able to turn from side to side until the prophetic act was completed (see verse 8). Ezekiel indeed became one with his message.

Perhaps Ezekiel's most difficult test of obedience, as we noted in chapter 3, came in the wake of his wife's death. Although God's grace was surely sufficient, God would not allow Ezekiel to mourn. God told him to groan silently, not to wail at her grave, not to uncover his head or take off his sandals, not to perform any of the typical rituals of mourning or to even accept food his consoling friends brought (see Ezekiel 24:15–18). Ezekiel became a sign to the people of how they should respond in the face of impending doom.

Once again, Ezekiel became one with his message.

The Power of Transparency

When you get to know the Old Testament prophets, you see a running theme: They not only became one with their message, but were transparent. Jeremiah was known as the weeping prophet because we see his heart in his ministry. Moses did not try to hide his struggles in prophetically leading Israel through the wilderness. David was perhaps the most transparent prophet of all, openly recording his emotions, struggles and victories in the Psalms for future generations to read and learn from.

I generally do not share a blow-by-blow description of my life as it is happening—mostly because I need to digest a lesson in order to share it—but I am very transparent in my writing because it helps people. I have often been tempted not to speak so boldly due to the backlash I invariably get from some who are convicted by the message. But, as I shared in a previous chapter, early on in my ministry the Holy Spirit led me to Ezekiel 3:18:

> "When I say to the wicked, 'You shall surely die,' and you give him no warning, nor speak to warn the wicked from his wicked way, to save his life, that same wicked man shall die in his iniquity; but his blood I will require at your hand."

Prophetic ministry is not about popularity. The work the Holy Spirit does in you prepares you to serve others. Your prophetic ministry is an expression of what the Holy Spirit has delivered you from, what He has done in you and what He is impressing upon your heart. It is about your experience. You learn the truth the Lord wants you to deliver through practical experience, and then you demonstrate it by walking it out—all before you ever preach it. God has to take you through a message before you can share it with the right spirit.

This is how you become one with your message. Going through the wilderness breaks you and leaves you with a humbler heart. From that position, you can speak the truth boldly—and in love.

22

Mastering Ministering in Love

I will never forget it. A visiting prophet from Europe was ministering at a church conference, and the altar was filled with saints looking for a prophetic word. I watched for nearly an hour as he rebuked people one by one for their shortcomings and mistakes. That was not my experience of the prophetic, and it was certainly not ministering in love.

I was troubled. But I became more troubled when he prophesied over me.

I was a young prophetic minister at the time in the church culture I mentioned earlier—the one that dictated blind obedience to spiritual leadership. I knew that I would be rebuked either way—if I went up to the line or if I did not go up to the line—so I went up hoping for the best. It was a disaster. He spoke nothing but death over me. When I walked back to my seat I was covered in witchcraft.

That was a hard lesson to learn, but I am glad I learned it when I did, because the temptation to follow man instead of what you know in your spirit to be true reemerges at strategic points in the prophet's walk.

That misguided prophet had forgotten Paul's guidelines for "the simple gift of prophecy," which is usually personal prophecy, offered in 1 Corinthians 14:3: edification, exhortation and comfort. God can and does use prophets to speak individual words of correction or realignment, but it is not usually done in a prayer line with a microphone so all can hear. One of my early prophetic mentors had the grace to offer strong words of personal correction that left you walking away with a thankful heart because you felt the love in it. Correction is part of prophetic ministry, but personal words are for the "upbuilding and constructive spiritual progress and encouragement and consolation" (1 Corinthians 14:3 AMPLIFIED). Personal prophecy is not for blasting people.

A mature prophet understands how to minister the Spirit in love. After all, God is love. To minister out of anything but love is to fail miserably. Paul outlines the characteristics of a mature prophet in 1 Corinthians 13, the love chapter. In it, Paul offers prophetic insight into God's heart that every prophet would do well to heed. He offers a balanced perspective on prophetic ministry, or any other ministry that manifests God's supernatural power.

The "Useless Nobodies"

If God has called you into prophetic ministry, you should feel intense hunger to manifest the gifts of the Spirit for the glory of God—but you should also crave maturity. Want to know how to get through the making process faster? Walk in love. That is the message in 1 Corinthians 13. When true prophecy manifests, it manifests in love. Prophets who walk in love—who are patient, kind, not envious, not boastful or proud, not dishonoring others, not self-seeking, not easily angered, quick to forgive, not delighting in evil but rejoicing in truth, protecting, trusting, hoping and persevering—cannot ultimately fail. And they will grow in grace and maturity much more quickly.

Keep in mind that the Bible was not written in chapters. Paul's thoughts in 1 Corinthians 12 did not close at the beginning of 1 Corinthians 13. This was one letter. With that understanding, consider that the last verse in 1 Corinthians 12 says this: "Earnestly desire and zealously cultivate the greatest and best gifts and graces (the higher gifts and the choicest graces). And yet I will show you a still more excellent way [one that is better by far and the highest of them all—love]" (verse 31 AMPLIFIED).

Paul broke it down with practical examples of various ministries flowing in love. He spoke to the charismatic and Pentecostal camps when he wrote:

> If I [can] speak in the tongues of men and [even] of angels, but have not love (that reasoning, intentional, spiritual devotion such as is inspired by God's love for and in us), I am only a noisy gong or a clanging cymbal.
>
> 1 Corinthians 13:1 AMPLIFIED

Prophets are supposed to blow the trumpet, not be a noisy gong or a clanging cymbal. Without love, prophets are making the wrong noise. Paul continued:

> And if I have prophetic powers (the gift of interpreting the divine will and purpose), and understand all the secret truths and mysteries and possess all knowledge, and if I have [sufficient] faith so that I can remove mountains, but have not love (God's love in me) I am nothing (a useless nobody).
>
> 1 Corinthians 13:2 AMPLIFIED

He is speaking right to the prophetic and faith camps now. Most prophets I know have passion to be "a voice," but if they fail to minister in love they will be useless nobodies, from a Kingdom perspective.

Paul went on to say: "Even if I dole out all that I have [to the poor in providing] food, and if I surrender my body to be burned or in order that I may glory, but have not love (God's love in me), I gain nothing" (1 Corinthians 13:3 AMPLIFIED). Prophets should be looking for eternal rewards in heaven, not the short-term rewards of man. If what you do in thought, word and deed is not motivated by love, do not bother doing it. Spend more time with God until you can move in the right spirit.

Ministering in Love

Some say the prophetic voice has a hard edge. That may be so—but only when dealing with devils. When dealing with people, mature prophets walk in love. Let's continue looking at 1 Corinthians 13:4–8 (from the Amplified Bible) as it relates to a mature prophetic ministry.

1. "Love endures long and is patient and kind." A mature prophet who walks in love does not get bent out of shape because he delivered a prophetic word to the pastor about a new building project two years ago and nobody has taken action yet. Once you have delivered a prophetic word, your job is to pray and be patient. You cannot control whether or not a person receives it or takes action on it. I used to get frustrated because I would deliver prophecies to my local church leader and nothing would happen for years—but eventually they took action. It is a matter of timing. And the timing is in God's hands. When you release the word, your job is to keep it in prayer—not try to force it through.

2. "Love never is envious nor boils over with jealousy." In other words, the prophet who walks in love is not comparing herself to other prophets and is not jealous because another prophet got invited up on the platform to prophesy or preach. If you are walking in envy and jealousy, you are not ready to get up on the platform and prophesy or preach. You need to mature in love first.

3. Love "is not boastful or vainglorious, does not display itself haughtily. It is not conceited (arrogant and inflated with pride)." You have probably seen prophets who walk in pride. They think they are more anointed or somehow better than everyone else. That is not love.

4. Love "is not rude (unmannerly) and does not act unbecomingly. Love (God's love in us) does not insist on its own rights or its own way, for it is not self-seeking." Some prophets get offended if you do not use their titles when you address them. That is not a mature prophet. Jesus' followers did not address Him as "Prophet Jesus." The same goes for the Old Testament prophets. It has been said that the prophet makes the title; the title does not make the prophet. There is nothing wrong with a title, per se; it is when you crave or demand one that you show your lack of maturity.

5. Love "is not touchy or fretful or resentful; it takes no account of the evil done to it [it pays no attention to a suffered wrong]." If you are going to move in prophetic ministry, you will need thick skin and a big heart. I think that all the "cursing and judgment" prophets have resentment in their hearts. They paid attention to a suffered wrong, and their flow is bitter. Cursing and blessing cannot come from the same mouth (see James 3:10).

6. Love "does not rejoice at injustice and unrighteousness, but rejoices when right and truth prevail." In other words, love does not rejoice to send out email detailing the prophetic words received before the disaster happened. Let me mention again that when Hurricane Katrina hit New Orleans, some prophets literally bragged about how they "predicted God's wrath," and some were competing to be known as the one who prophesied it first. They were rejoicing in calamity. In like manner, some prophesy a disaster that does not come, and then take credit for praying all night to break it. That is not love.

7. "Love bears up under anything and everything that comes, is ever ready to believe the best of every person, its hopes

are fadeless under all circumstances, and it endures everything [without weakening]. Love never fails [never fades out or becomes obsolete or comes to an end]." This is the picture of the mature prophet. Mature prophets bear up under anything that comes their way—and still honor God in the process. They believe the best of every person and work with others to see them set free in the name of Jesus.

It Is Time to Grow Up

It is time to grow up. Right after expounding on the virtues of walking in love, the apostle Paul exhorts us to put away childish things (see 1 Corinthians 13:11). What is a childish thing? One perspective is this: anything that prevents you from walking in love. That could be jealousy, pride, control or some other ungodly character trait that you need to renounce. Love will deliver you from all of that and more, if you let it.

Love will also safeguard your calling. Think about it. If you are walking in love, you are going to be obedient. If you are walking in love, you are not going to merchandise God's word for His people. If you are walking in love, you are going to be humble. If you are walking in love you are going to be gentle. The fruit of the Spirit is going to manifest in your life alongside the spiritual gifts.

If you want to get through the making process with fewer bumps and bruises, major in the major instead of majoring in the minor. If you have the choice of spending more time with the Holy Spirit cultivating a love walk or going to a conference about how to fight devils and prophesy better, choose love. When you do, everything else will fall into place. You will have a more accurate prophetic flow and more spiritual authority. You will be more dangerous to the kingdom of darkness and more profitable for the Kingdom of Light. And you will heap up eternal rewards.

Remember, the making process never ends. You might say that it is always time to grow up. Prophecy will be fulfilled and pass away; tongues will cease; knowledge will be superseded by truth. Only actions motivated by love will count for anything in eternity. Paul writes:

> And so faith, hope, love abide [faith—conviction and belief respecting man's relation to God and divine things; hope—joyful and confident expectation of eternal salvation; love—true affection for God and man, growing out of God's love for and in us], these three; but the greatest of these is love.
>
> 1 Corinthians 13:13 Amplified

A Prophetic Prayer

I want to leave this prayer with you. This is my prayer for all those who read the book. You can pray this over yourself.

Thank You, God, that You are love. I commit myself today to walk in the love of the Father. I thank You that Your Spirit, dwelling in me, empowers me to walk in love. Thank You, Lord, that You teach me day by day, hour by hour, how to receive more of Your love, how to love You more and how to show love to others. Give me an anointing to love.

Father, show me where I am failing to walk in love. Show me how to get into alignment with Your love. Break off the impurities in my soul. Break off the pride. Break off the disobedience. Break off the rebellion. Break me in the name of Jesus so that I may grow into the stature of Christ and be more profitable for Your Kingdom.

I put my trust in You, Lord. I climb onto Your potter's wheel, and I know that I am safe in Your capable hands. You will not put more pressure on me than I can bear. I know that no matter how fast I am spinning or how hot the kiln gets, You are with me. I submit myself to You, and I resist the enemy. Help me discern the difference between Your hand and the enemy's attacks.

I lay myself bare before You, Lord. Teach me. Train me. Strip from me every sinful characteristic, every sinful thought, and help me renew my mind in the name of Jesus and for Your glory. Amen.

Index